NOMADIC FURNITURE 2

ALSO BY THE SAME AUTHORS:

DESIGN FOR THE REAL WORLD, PANTHEON BOOKS, 1971
NOMADIC FURNITURE 1 — WITH JAMES HENNESSEY, PANTHEON
BOOKS, 1973
"BIG CHARACTER" POSTER: WORK CHART FOR
DESIGNERS, FINN SLOTH, POSTBOX 51, DK-2920 CHARLOTTENLUND,
DENMARK, 1973

More about→ HOW TO BUILD AND WHERE TO BUY LIGHTWEIGHT FURNITURE THAT FOLDS, COLLAPSES, STACKS, KNOCKS DOWN, INFLATES OR CAN BE THROWN AWAY BUT BE RECYCLED. BEING BOTH A BOOK OF INSTRUCTION AND A CATALOG OF ACCESS FOR EASY MOVING

NOMADIC FURNITURE 2

BY JAMES HENNESSEY AND VICTOR PAPANEK, WITH MANY EASY-TO-FOLLOW DIAGRAMS, PHOTOGRAPHS & DRAWINGS BY THE AUTHORS.

PANTHEON BOOKS
A DIVISION OF RANDOM HOUSE, NEW YORK

ALL RIGHTS RESERVED UNDER INTERNATIONAL AND PAN-AMERICAN
COPYRIGHT CONVENTIONS. PUBLISHED IN THE UNITED STATES BY
PANTHEON BOOKS, A DIVISION OF RANDOM HOUSE, INC., NEW YORK,
AND SIMULTANEOUSLY IN CANADA BY RANDOM HOUSE OF CANADA
LIMITED, TORONTO.

LIBRARY OF CONGRESS CATALOGING IN PUBLICATION DATA
HENNESSEY, JAMES
NOMADIC FURNITURE 2.

AT HEAD OF TITLE: MORE ABOUT HOW TO BUILD AND WHERE TO BUY
LIGHTWEIGHT FURNITURE THAT FOLDS, COLLAPSES, STACKS, KNOCKS
DOWN, INFLATES, OR CAN BE THROWN AWAY BUT BE RECYCLED.
BEING BOTH A BOOK OF INSTRUCTION AND A CATALOG OF ACCESS
FOR EASY MOVING.

1. FURNITURE MAKING — AMATEURS' MANUALS. 2. FURNITURE —
CATALOGS.   I. PAPANEK, VICTOR J., JOINT AUTHOR.
II. TITLE.   TT195 .H47   684.1   73-18725
ISBN: 0-394-48563-7
ISBN: 0-394-70638-2 (PBK.)

MANUFACTURED IN THE UNITED STATES OF AMERICA
 9 8 7 6 5 4 3 2
 FIRST EDITION

table of contents:

introduction:

<u>Now you are even more nomadic</u>: SINCE WE WROTE OUR EARLIER VOLUME LAST YEAR, STATISTICS FROM WASHINGTON TEND TO SHOW THAT NOW AMERICANS MAKE MAJOR MOVES & RELOCATE EVERY 18 MONTHS TO TWO YEARS. → WE ALL LIVE IN A WORLD of 1-YEAR LEASES, 3-MONTH FASHIONS, AND JOBS THAT MAY MEAN RELOCATION EVERY FEW MONTHS. TO THOSE OF US IN THE "FLOATING ACADEMIC CRAP-GAME" (PROFESSORS), "FOREVER" IS A 9-MONTH APPOINTMENT. <u>AND YET</u>: WE TRY TO LIVE WITH ORDER & BEAUTY of OUR OWN MAKING, BUT WITHOUT GIVING UP OUR FLEXIBILITY. EVEN "SETTLING DOWN" SMACKS of SPLIT-LEVEL BOREDOM IN SUBURBIA, TWO JAGUARS AND A WIFE WITH BLUE-RINSED HAIR; OF ANXIETY, ULCERS AND ERODING STATUS. AND NOT JUST IN THE U.S. VIC HAS SPENT THE LAST YEAR IN EUROPE AND FOUND A SIMILAR DESIRE FOR A NOMADIC LIFE-STYLE AMONG YOUNG PEOPLE IN AFRICA, ENGLAND, GERMANY, THE

SCANDINAVIAN COUNTRIES & IN EASTERN EUROPE.

Why we wrote a second volume: WHEN WE HAD
FINISHED OUR EARLIER BOOK IN AUGUST 1972,
WE HOPED OTHERS WOULD CARRY OUR CONCEPTS FURTHER;
WE EXPECTED A RASH OF BOOKS DEALING WITH BUILDING
& BUYING THINGS THAT CAN BE MOVED EASILY. IT HAS
NOT HAPPENED YET. ➔ _On the other hand_ WE HAVE
RECEIVED NEARLY A THOUSAND LETTERS IN LESS THAN
SIX MONTHS FROM READERS WHO BUILT SOME OF OUR
DESIGNS & ASKED FOR MORE. SEVERAL GOOD IDEAS
CAME FROM READERS OF OUR FIRST BOOK; YOU'LL FIND
THEM FURTHER ON. INDUSTRY TOO HAS SEEN THE NEED
FOR LIGHTWEIGHT, EASY-TO-MOVE FURNITURE & YOU
WILL FIND MANY OF THEIR DESIGNS, WITH OURS, IN
THE FOLLOWING PAGES.

Our design philosophy: WE FEEL THAT MUCH
IS WRONG IN OUR SOCIETY AND THAT SEEKING REFUGE
IN SLEEK OBJECTS IS A COP-OUT. THE SCREECHING
TV COMMERCIALS AND THE NON-STOP ASSAULT ON
OUR SENSES VIA BILLBOARDS & ADVERTISEMENTS
HAVE LED MANY TO A REVULSION FROM THE MERE

OWNING of MATERIAL THINGS. THE RISING WAVE of CRIME [and with that: rising insurance rates] MAKES IT SILLY TO FURNISH OUR APARTMENTS WITH COSTLY POS~ SESSIONS THAT MAY BE SMASHED or STOLEN, ONCE WE GO OUT FOR THE EVENING. PEOPLE ARE ALSO INCREASINGLY AWARE of HOW THEY HAVE BEEN MANIPULATED BY FASHION. YOUNG PEOPLE ESPECIALLY HAVE TURNED AROUND CLOTHING AND THEIR NEEDS FOR FURNITURE, SO THAT UNCLUTTERED PERSONAL FREEDOM BECOMES THE GOAL, RATHER THAN AN OBJECT~LADEN SHOWPLACE.

<u>Have we ripped off ideas?</u> WHENEVER WE FEEL THAT A COMMERCIAL SOLUTION WORKS WELL, WE TELL YOU WHERE IT CAN BE BOUGHT. BUT IF WE FEEL THAT YOU CAN IMPROVE or ADAPT A DESIGN. ➡ <u>OUR OWN OR ANYONE ELSE's</u>, WE SAY SO. REMEMBER: YOU ARE NOT READING A BOOK ABOUT DESIGN. RATHER, THIS IS A BOOK TO DEMYTHOLOGIZE DESIGN & MAKE IT AVAILABLE TO PEOPLE. IF YOU ARE NOT A PROFESSIONAL ARCHITECT or DESIGNER, THEN THIS BOOK WAS WRITTEN FOR YOU. WHEN OUR FIRST VOLUME

APPEARED, ONE NEWSPAPER SAID: »IT IS THE ONLY BOOK WITH EQUAL APPEAL FOR READERS of *THE EAST VILLAGE OTHER* AND *FAMILY CIRCLE* ...« IF WE CAN SUCCEED IN BRINGING SUCH DIFFERING CONSTITUENCIES TOGETHER, WE'RE SATISFIED. A FEW DESIGNERS HAVE COMPLAINED THAT WE HAVE "TOO FEW GREAT, RADICAL SOLUTIONS." THAT IS A MISPERCEPTION OF WHAT OUR BOOKS ARE ABOUT: WE TRY TO MAKE SIMPLE IDEAS [THAT WORK] AVAILABLE BROADLY. THE DESIGN ESTABLISHMENT PRESS HAS QUITE PROPERLY IGNORED *NOMADIC FURNITURE*, ONE WOULD HARDLY EXPECT ANAESTHESIOLOGISTS TO APPLAUD BOOKS ON NATURAL CHILDBIRTH METHODS.

Why not just things to build? BECAUSE SOME THINGS [A DESK CHAIR, FOR INSTANCE] ARE DIFFICULT FOR THOSE UNFAMILIAR WITH TOOLS. BECAUSE LIVING IN A KLEENEX CULTURE, WE MUST LEARN TO THROW LESS AWAY & MAKE DO WITH RECYCLED OLDER THINGS. BECAUSE WOOD IS SCARCE, WILL BE SCARCER STILL & COSTS MORE. BECAUSE SOME INDUSTRIAL PRODUCTS ARE MUCH BETTER & CHEAPER THAN ANYTHING WE MIGHT DESIGN FOR "DO-IT-YOURSELF" METHODS. BECAUSE THERE ARE PEOPLE WHO COULDN'T BUILD A TABLE IF THEY TRIED.

WE DEDICATE THIS BOOK TO ALL OF YOU WHO ARE STILL CHOOSING INSTEAD OF THINKING YOU KNOW, <u>TRAVELLING INSTEAD</u> OF FEELING YOU HAVE ARRIVED, <u>FINDING YOURSELVES</u> INSTEAD OF SETTLING DOWN.

KØBENHAVN ~ KYOTO ~ BRAMHALL, CHESHIRE
1972-73

VALENCIA
1972-73

P.S.: UNLIKE THE "POSITIVELY LAST FAREWELL APPEARANCE" OF AN AGING PRIMADONNA, THERE WILL BE NO <u>NOMADIC FURNITURE 3</u>. <u>YOU</u> WRITE IT!

Note: ALL MEASUREMENTS ARE GIVEN IN INCHES. THICKNESS OF PLYWOOD, PARTICLE BOARD & CHIP BOARD, <u>UNLESS OTHERWISE STATED</u>, IS 3/4".

THE SIGN: ∅ MEANS DIAMETER OF A CIRCLE. THUS: ∅36" IS A CIRCLE THREE FEET ACROSS.

on human measure:

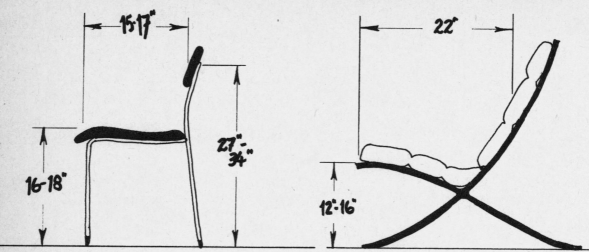

15-17"
16-18"
27"-34"
22"
12"-16"

AS WE SAID IN OUR EARLIER VOLUME: THESE SIZES ARE ONLY APPROXIMATIONS → MEASURE YOURSELF & YOUR FAMILY. IN VARIOUS PARTS OF THE WORLD, HUMAN MEASURE DIFFERS RADICALLY. LITTLE

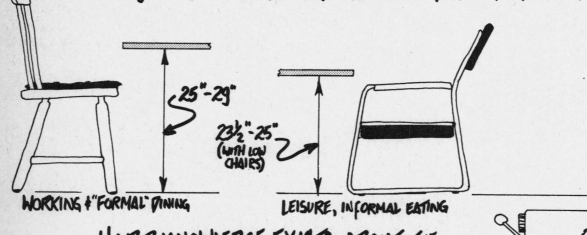

25"-29"

23½"-25" (WITH LOW CHAIRS)

WORKING & "FORMAL" DINING   LEISURE, INFORMAL EATING

HARD KNOWLEDGE EXISTS ABOUT THE ELDERLY, CHILDREN & WOMEN ESPECIALLY.

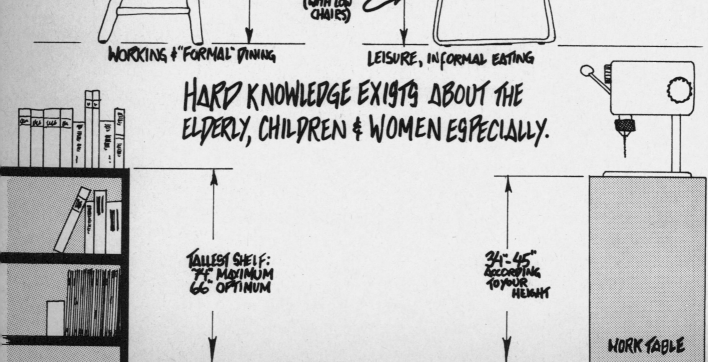

TALLEST SHELF:
74" MAXIMUM
66" OPTIMUM

34"-45"
ACCORDING TO YOUR HEIGHT

WORK TABLE

CONVENTIONAL TABLE SIZES:

CIRCULAR:

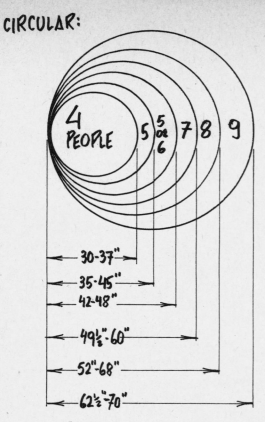

RECTANGULAR:

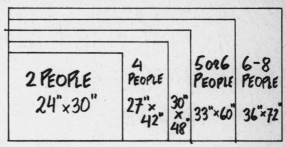

SQUARE:

2 PEOPLE
24"□ or
30"□

4 PEOPLE
30" – 36"□

VIC HAS HOWEVER RECEIVED A VERY HELPFUL LETTER FROM JOHN RHOUDS, RESEARCH ASSISTANT, DEPTS. OF SOMATOLOGY & MEDICAL ANTHROPOLOGY, PEABODY MUSEUM, HARVARD. HE SUGGESTS THE FOLLOWING FOLLOW-UP MATERIAL [IF ERGONOMICS IS YOUR THING]:

P. BAKER & J.S. WEINER: *THE BIOLOGY OF HUMAN ADAPTABILITY*, CLARENDON PRESS, OXFORD, 1966

[FOR U.S., NATIVE AMERICANS, LATINOS, AFRICANS, EAST INDIANS, MANY ASIAN & PACIFIC GROUPS]

J.M. TANNER: *GROWTH AT ADOLESCENCE*, BLACKWELL, OXFORD, 1962

JUAN COMAS: *MANUAL OF PHYSICAL ANTHROPOLOGY*, C.C. THOMAS, SPRINGFIELD, ILL. 1960

[FOR BABIES, CHILDREN & GROWTH STUDIES]

JOHN RHOUDS GOES ON TO SAY THAT: "ELDERLY AMERICAN MEN HAVE BEEN MEASURED FOR THE NORMATIVE AGING STUDY OF THE VETERANS' ADMINISTRATION. MEASUREMENTS ON A WELL-DESIGNED POPULATION SAMPLE OF AMERICAN WOMEN WERE MADE IN THE NATL. HEALTH EXAMINATION SURVEY [AVAILABLE FROM THE NATL. CENTER FOR HEALTH STATISTICS, US. PUBLIC HEALTH SURVEY SERVICE, WASHINGTON]. WOMEN IN GENERAL, THOUGH, ARE STILL THE MOST CONSPICUOUSLY UNDERMEASURED GROUP..."

SEATiNG:

IF SITTING COMFORTABLY WERE EVEN REMOTELY POSSIBLE, THERE WOULDN'T BE 25,000 DIFFERENT CHAIRS TO CHOOSE FROM.

ALL SITTING IS COMPROMISE. BY MAKING A LIFE-CAST of YOUR ASS, A DESIGNER CAN MAKE ONE CHAIR [PERSONALLY FITTED TO YOU] IN WHICH YOU [AND YOU ONLY] CAN BE SUPREMELY COMFORTABLE IF YOU DON'T CHANGE POSITION, EVER.... THERE'S THE RUB: WE ARE COMFORTABLE ONLY IF WE CAN FIDGET, MOVE AROUND IN OUR CHAIRS, AND TRY TO DISCOVER A THIRD WAY OF CROSSING OUR LEGS.

SO ALL CHAIRS ARE [MORE or LESS] UNI-POSITIONAL LIKE MOST DINING CHAIRS, or ELSE MULTI-POSITIONAL LIKE LOUNGING PADS, THE SACK or A WING-BACK, CHINTZ-COVERED LIBRARY CHAIR IN COLONIAL WILLIAMSBURG.

BASICALLY WE CAN SIT ON ALMOST ANYTHING. AND THAT IS THE REASON WHY SO MANY CONTEMPORARY DESIGNERS [WITH ITALY IN THE FOREFRONT] HAVE

MASSAGED THEIR OWN EGOS BY CONFECTING CHAIRS THAT LOOK LIKE: A NET of ORANGE FOOTBALLS; A SPIKY CUBE; A MURDER VICTIM'S TORSO WRAPPED IN PLASTIC & ROPE; A TRANSPARENT BEACH CHAIR; OR A KINKY [FAINTLY SURGICAL] RUBBER & STEEL CONTRAPTION THAT HOLDS APPEAL ONLY FOR THOSE VASTLY LEARNED IN THE REMOTEST AREAS of SADO-MASOCHIST FETISHISM.

TRENDY DESIGNERS HAVE TOLD US FOR 60 YEARS TO SIT LOW [WHAT ABOUT GRANDPARENTS or IN-LAWS, TRYING TO GET UP?]; OTHERS FEEL WE MUST SIT MINIMALLY [THIN SHEETS of PLASTIC SUPPORTED BY KNIFE-EDGED ALUMINUM PROFILES: WHAT IF WE HAVE FAT FRIENDS?] or ELSE WE ARE PERSUADED TO FILL OUR LIVING ROOM WITH A MASS of COVERED FOAM CONSTRUCTS WHICH WILL SLEEP SIXTEEN PEOPLE IN REMARKABLE POSITIONS - BUT STILL NOT ANSWER THE PROBLEM of SITTING.

ADDED TO THIS ARE CULTURAL CHANGES: THE "PROPER" UPRIGHT POSTURE [BACK *NEVER* TOUCHING THE BACK REST] HAS BEEN SUCCEEDED BY VARYING RECLINING & SPRAWLING POSITIONS.

➡ WE HAVE TAKEN THE SAME VIEW AS IN OUR EARLIER
BOOK: SOME SEATING UNITS [ESPECIALLY WORKING &
DINING CHAIRS] ARE DIFFICULT TO BUILD &
CAN BE BOUGHT INEXPENSIVELY OR USED.
WE HAVE LISTED THOSE THAT SEEM TO
MAKE THE MOST SENSE.

• OTHER UNITS CAN BE BUILT QUITE EASILY
AND INEXPENSIVELY AND STILL BE NOMADIC.
THIS HOLDS TRUE ESPECIALLY OF "SOFA"-LIKE
AND "DAY BED"-TYPE UNITS, AS WELL AS
RELAXING CHAIRS.

More important:

REMEMBER AGAIN THAT EVERYTHING IN THIS BOOK SHOULD
ONLY SERVE AS A SPRINGBOARD FOR YOUR OWN IMAGINATION.
DON'T JUST BLINDLY BUILD OR BUY WHAT WE SUGGEST:
SEE IF YOU CAN IMPROVE OR RETHINK IT FIRST.

REMEMBER ALSO THAT THIS BOOK IS NO EXHAUSTIVE CATA-
LOG OF EVERY NOMADIC CHAIR. WE MAY WELL HAVE LEFT
OUT SOME IMPORTANT PIECES, BUT _YOU_ CAN ADD &
SEARCH AS WELL. GOOD LUCK!

DOUBLE-BOLSTER SLING CHAIR:

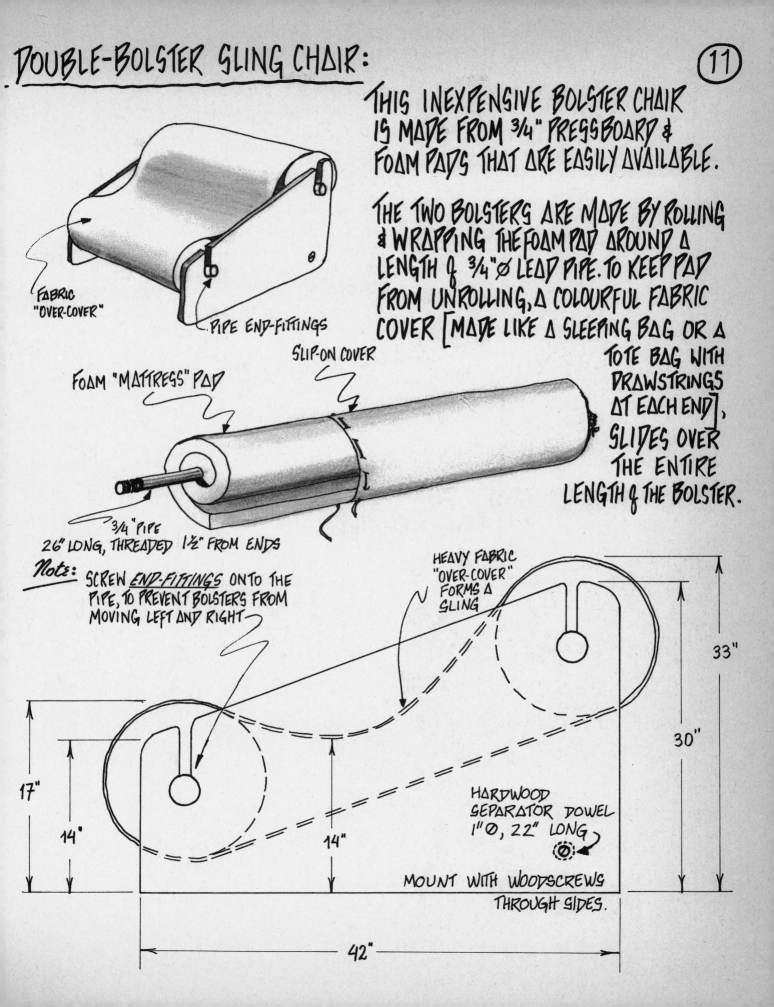

THIS INEXPENSIVE BOLSTER CHAIR IS MADE FROM 3/4" PRESSBOARD & FOAM PADS THAT ARE EASILY AVAILABLE.

THE TWO BOLSTERS ARE MADE BY ROLLING & WRAPPING THE FOAM PAD AROUND A LENGTH of 3/4" Ø LEAD PIPE. TO KEEP PAD FROM UNROLLING, A COLOURFUL FABRIC COVER [MADE LIKE A SLEEPING BAG OR A TOTE BAG WITH DRAWSTRINGS AT EACH END], SLIDES OVER THE ENTIRE LENGTH of THE BOLSTER.

FABRIC "OVER-COVER"

PIPE END-FITTINGS

SLIP-ON COVER

FOAM "MATTRESS" PAD

3/4" PIPE 26" LONG, THREADED 1½" FROM ENDS

Note: SCREW *END-FITTINGS* ONTO THE PIPE, TO PREVENT BOLSTERS FROM MOVING LEFT AND RIGHT

HEAVY FABRIC "OVER-COVER" FORMS A SLING

33"

30"

17"

14"

14"

HARDWOOD SEPARATOR DOWEL 1" Ø, 22" LONG

MOUNT WITH WOODSCREWS THROUGH SIDES.

42"

FOLD-DOWN DINING BENCH

WHILE IN DENMARK, VICTOR DESIGNED THIS SEATING UNIT FOR TWO. [YOU CAN MAKE IT WIDER, TO SEAT 3 or 4].

THE UNIT CAN BE MADE OUT of PINE, BEECH or WHATEVER. SEATS AND BEARING STRINGS ARE CANVAS, AS ARE THE PILLOWS [FILLED WITH SHREDDED FOAM]. THE ENTIRE UNIT IS GLUED AND SCREW~ASSEMBLED.

NINE LARGE EXPANSION SCREWS SECURELY ATTACH THE BENCH TO WALL STUDS.

Parts:

ALL 9 RAILS ARE MADE OF 1" THICK, 3" WIDE WOOD.

BESIDES THESE, YOU'LL NEED ③ WOODEN DOWELS, PINE, 1"∅. TWO WILL BE 50" LONG. THE ADJUSTING DOWEL NEEDS TO BE 54". PLUS CANVAS.

33"

3 PARTS "A" (BACK UPRIGHTS)

1"×3" CUTOFF

2 PARTS "B" (OUTSIDE SEAT RAILS)

1"×3" CUTOFF

18"

48"

3"

3"

2 PARTS "C" (BACK IN SETS)

2 PARTS "D" (FRONT & MID-SEAT RAIL)

50"

Assembly:

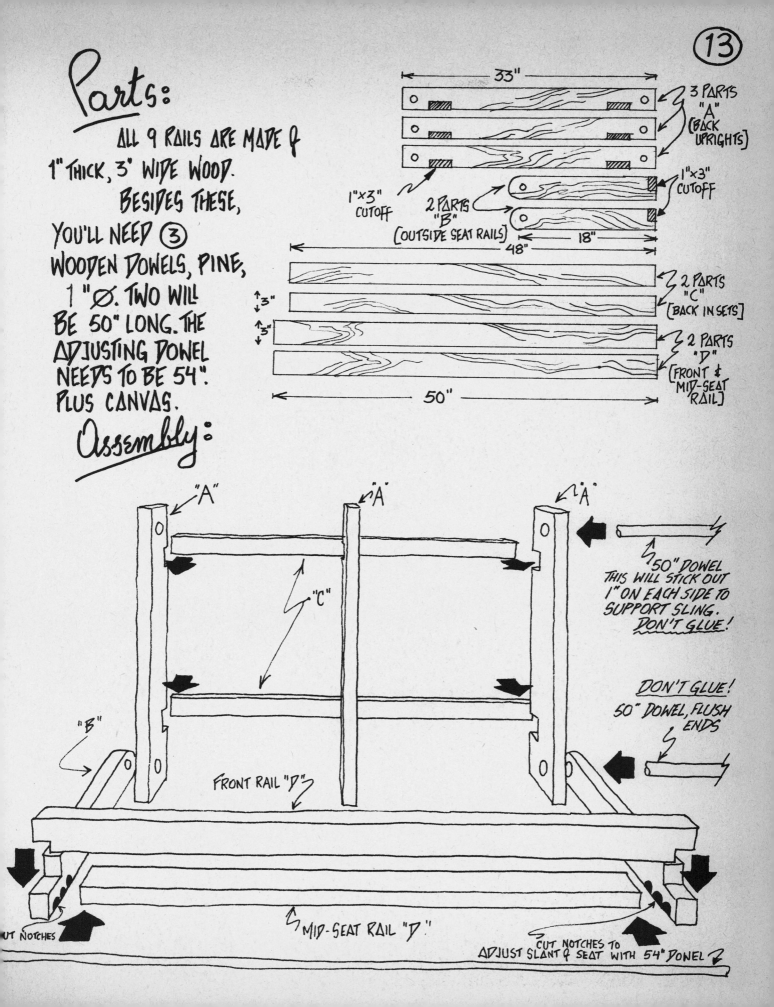

"A"

"A"

"A"

"C"

"B"

FRONT RAIL "D"

50" DOWEL THIS WILL STICK OUT 1" ON EACH SIDE TO SUPPORT SLING. DON'T GLUE!

DON'T GLUE! 50" DOWEL, FLUSH ENDS

CUT NOTCHES

MID-SEAT RAIL "D"

CUT NOTCHES TO ADJUST SLANT OF SEAT WITH 54" DOWEL

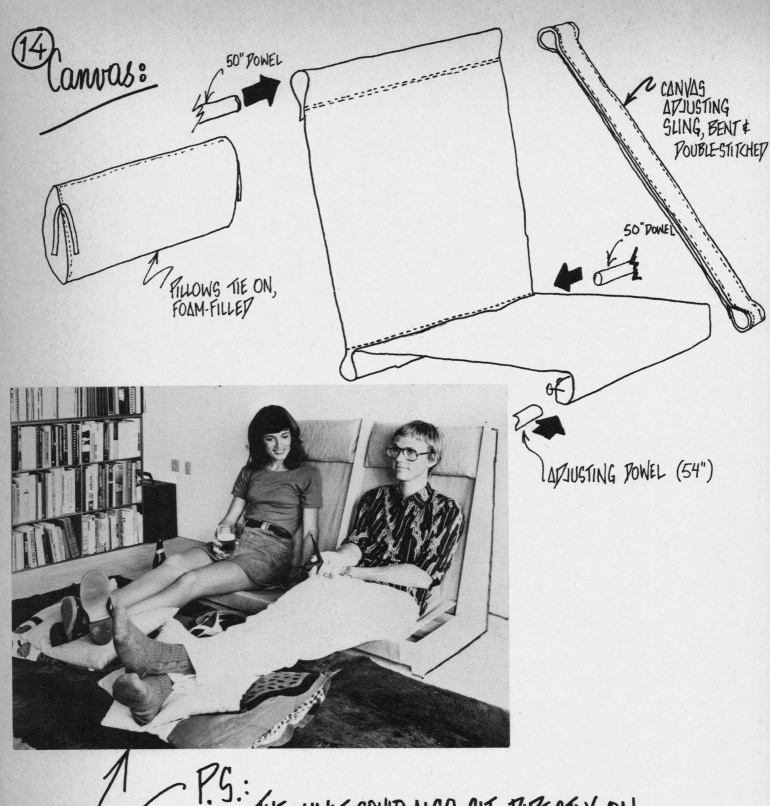

(14) Canvas:

50" DOWEL

PILLOWS TIE ON, FOAM-FILLED

CANVAS ADJUSTING SLING, BENT & DOUBLE-STITCHED

50" DOWEL

ADJUSTING DOWEL (54")

P.S.: THE UNIT COULD ALSO SIT DIRECTLY ON THE FLOOR FOR PARTIES & RELAXING.

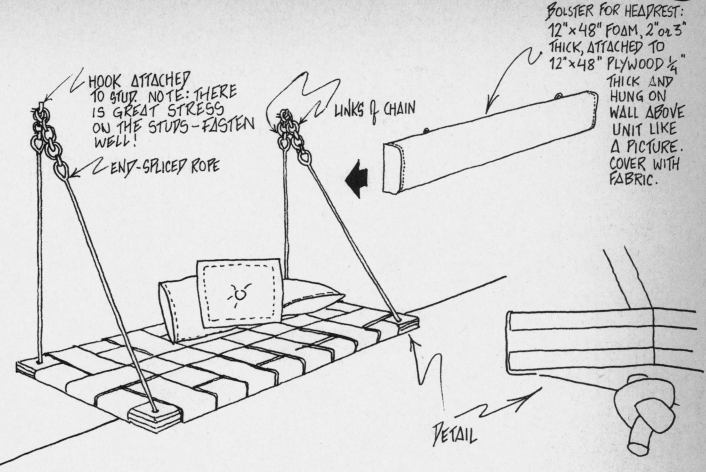

HOOK ATTACHED TO STUD. NOTE: THERE IS GREAT STRESS ON THE STUDS—FASTEN WELL!

LINKS OF CHAIN

END-SPLICED ROPE

BOLSTER FOR HEADREST: 12"x48" FOAM, 2"or3" THICK, ATTACHED TO 12"x48" PLYWOOD ¼" THICK AND HUNG ON WALL ABOVE UNIT LIKE A PICTURE. COVER WITH FABRIC.

DETAIL

SIMPLE WALL-HUNG SEAT:

THIS UNIT IS MADE of 2"x3" WOOD FOR THE FRAME & WEBBING. FRAME SIZES MIGHT BE 18"x48" or 24"x60". BE SURE TO USE REGULAR MARINE ROPE THAT, UNLIKE PLASTIC, DOESN'T STRETCH. ONCE CAREFULLY ADJUSTED THROUGH THE CHAIN LINKS, IT WON'T FLIP. ➤ MUCH ELSE CAN BE DONE USING THIS METHOD

LEAN-TO CHAIR:

VIC DEVELOPED THIS SUPPORT SYSTEM FOR BOOKS AT THE ASSUAN DAM CONFERENCE IN EGYPT & WE HAVE SHOWN IT ON PAGES 82-84 IN OUR EARLIER BOOK. NOW HE HAS TRIED THE SAME CONCEPT FOR NOMADIC SEATING ~ IT IS REMARKABLY STURDY & COMFORTABLE. YET MOVING IT MEANS ONLY

ROLLING UP THE CANVAS "BLIND" & CARRYING AN EMPTY FRAME. HERE ⟶ HARLANNE HAS UNROLLED THE BLIND ALMOST ALL THE WAY & SITS LOW. AS YOU CAN SEE, THE CANVAS

CAN BE INFINITELY ADJUSTED, JUST BY WINDING OR UNWINDING IT, AS WELL AS VARYING THE SLITS INTO WHICH THE TWO SQUARE RODS ARE INSERTED.

THE CHAIR RESTS AGAINST BOTH FLOOR & WALL & ESTABLISHES ENOUGH FRICTION NOT TO SLIDE. IF YOU'RE STILL UNWILLING TO TRUST IT, PUT 2 SMALL NAILS INTO THE WALL, JUST BELOW THE HORIZONTAL TOP-EDGE. IT CAN'T SLIDE NOW!

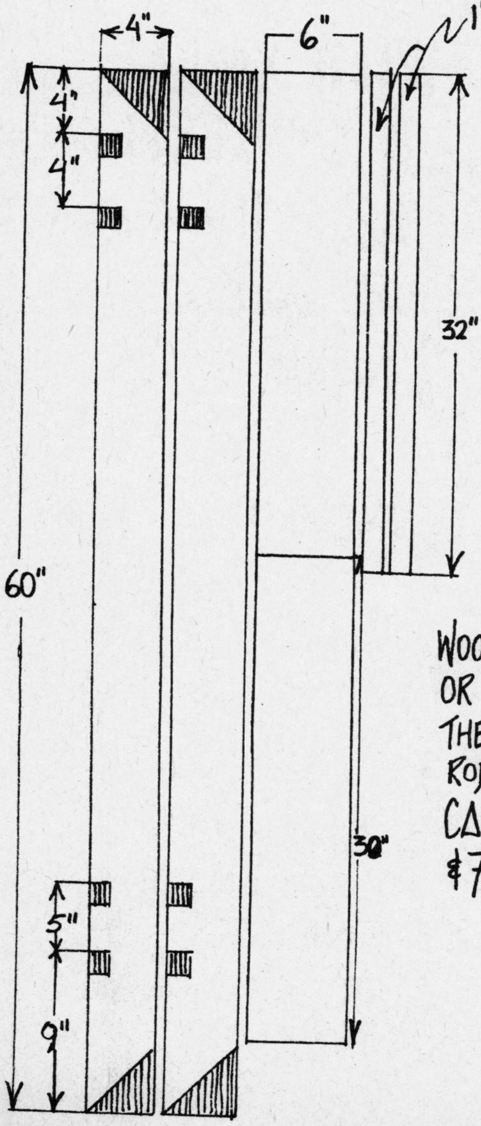

4"

6"

1"×1"

4"

4"

32"

60"

30"

WOOD IS 3/4" PLY OR 1" STOCK.
THE TWO 32" LONG RODS ARE 1"×1"
CANVAS IS 30" WIDE & 72" LONG.

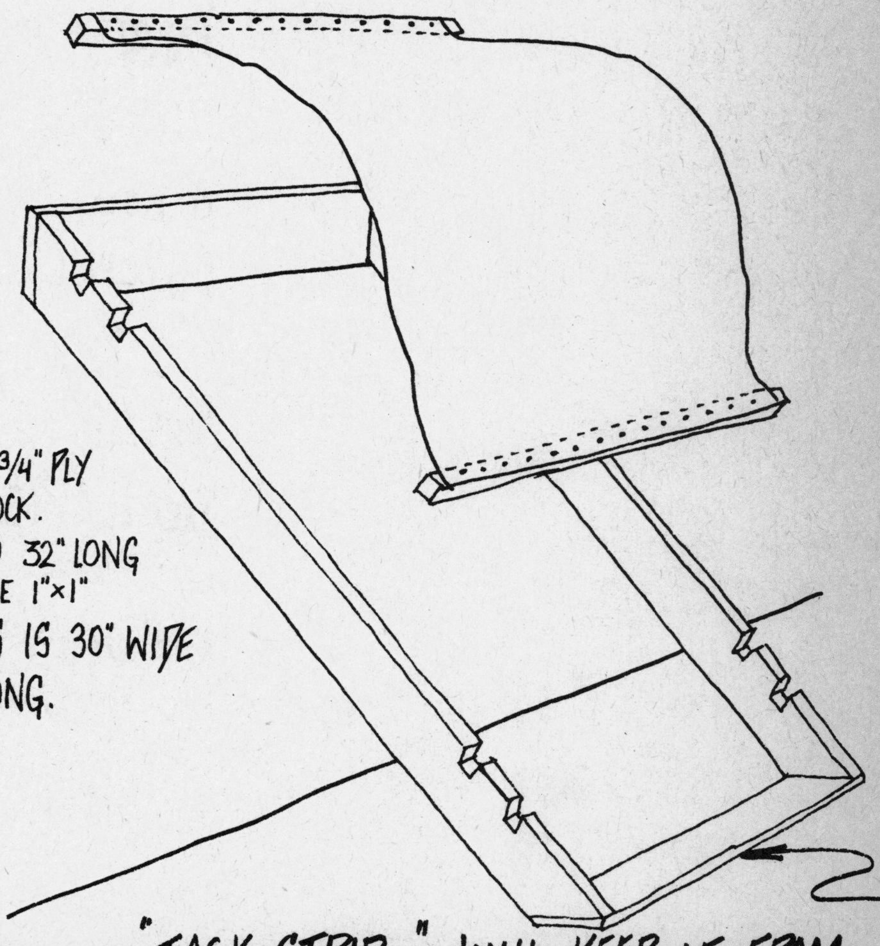

5"

9"

▦ MEANS: CUT OFF

"TACK STRIP" WILL KEEP IT FROM SLIDING ON A CARPET.

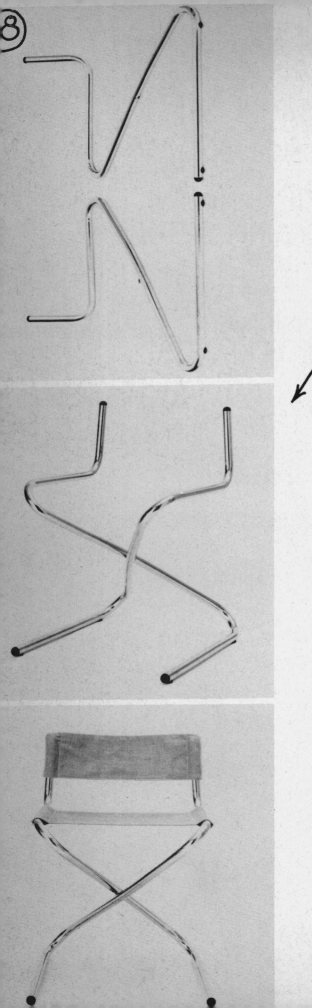

THERE ARE INNUMERABLE CHAIRS THAT FOLD. WE ARE LISTING ONLY THOSE THAT ARE INEXPENSIVE, STURDY, WELL~DESIGNED & NOMADIC.

THIS ONE WORKS WELL FOR DINING or DESK~WORK. IN SPITE of ITS COMPLETE KNOCK~DOWN FEATURES IT IS SURPRIS~INGLY COMFORTABLE. THE TUBULAR STRUCTURE SUPPORTS A SEAT & BACK of NATURAL LINEN CANVAS.

PRICE (IN DENMARK) ABOUT $27.-

AVAILABLE FROM:

KEVI & CO.
44 RUGVÆNGET,
2630 TAASTRUP, DENMARK
SHOWROOM: 3 FREDERIKSBERGGADE
            COPENHAGEN

A VERY COMFORTABLE
EASY CHAIR THAT KNOCKS
DOWN COMPLETELY.
BEECHWOOD & LINEN
CANVAS.
SMALL WRITING TABLETS
OR CORNER TABLETS
CAN BE ATTACHED TO
THE ARMS.
DESIGNED BY ROLF HEIDE
AVAILABLE FROM:
➡ WOHNBEDARF
   MITTELWEG 166
   2000 HAMBURG
   GERMANY

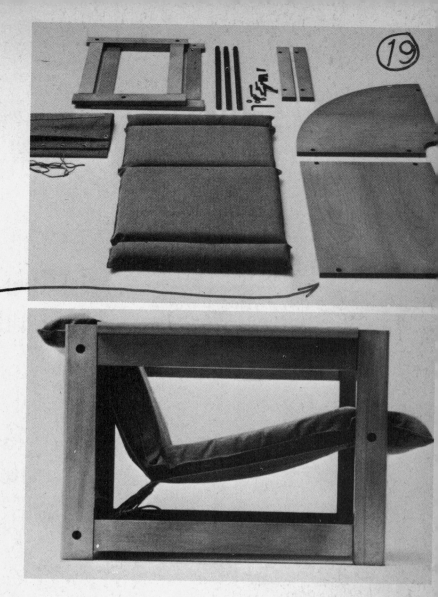

A DANISH RESTATEMENT
OF A DECK CHAIR. MADE OF
BEECHWOOD & CANVAS WITH
A REMOVABLE HEAD-CUSHION,
IT CAN BE USED INSIDE OR
OUTSIDE.
DESIGNED BY LAUGE VESTERGAARD
AVAILABLE FROM:
➡ CADO
   8200 AARHUS, DENMARK

AND SHOPS.

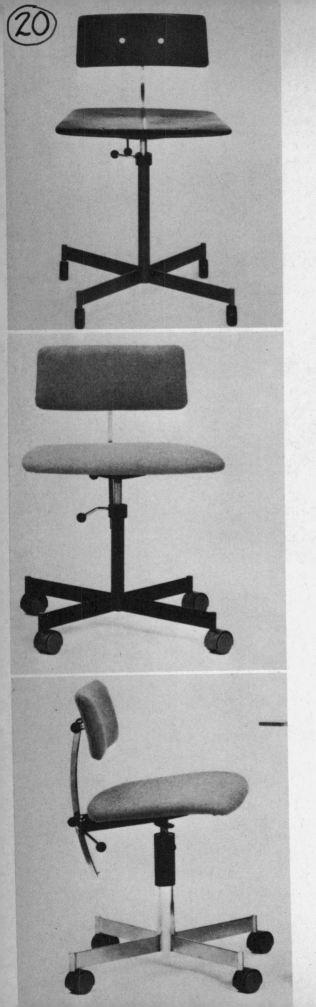

VICTOR DIVIDES HIS TIME EQUALLY BETWEEN TYPEWRITER & DRAFTING TABLE.

THE ONLY CHAIR THAT SEEMS TO CAUSE NO BACK-ACHES IS THIS ONE, WITH ALMOST INFINITE ADJUSTABILITY.

IN THE PLAIN WOODEN VERSION IT COSTS ABOUT $30.- AND COMES IN BRIGHT, ZIPPY COLOURS. THE UPHOLSTERED VERSION IS A LITTLE HIGHER. BOTH COME ON KEVI'S CASTERS [MORE ABOUT THEM ON PAGE 136].

DESIGN: ERIK MØLLER,
        IB & JØRGEN RASMUSSEN

AVAILABLE FROM:

KEVI
44 RUGVÆNGET
2630 TAASTRUP, DENMARK
SHOWROOM:
3 FREDERIKSBERGGADE
COPENHAGEN.

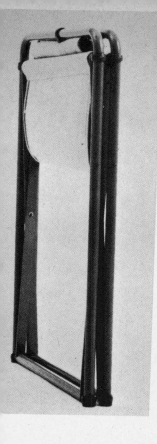

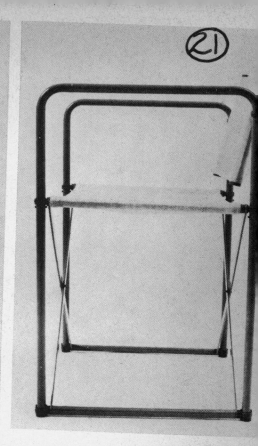

WE SPENT A GREAT DEAL of TIME IN OUR EARLIER BOOK, DISCUSSING THE MERITS of "DOUBLE~FUNCTION" CHAIRS, CHAIRS THAT SERVE EQUALLY WELL FOR DINING & DESK~WORK AS FOR OCCASIONAL RELAXING. BUT OUR RULES WERE ROUGHER: THE CHAIR ALSO HAD TO FOLD AND, FINALLY, BE EQUALLY USEFUL INDOORS or OUT. → ONLY TWO CHAIRS MET OUR STANDARDS WELL: A BEECH & LINEN CHAIR DESIGNED BY MOGENS KOCH IN THE EARLY THIRTIES AND THE "DIRECTOR'S CHAIR", GOING BACK 80 YEARS. NOW JØRGEN MØLLER HAS DESIGNED A NEW VERSION IN STAINLESS STEEL [EITHER CHROMED or WITH BRIGHT-LY COLOURED EPOXY BURNED INTO THE SURFACE TO KEEP IT RUST-FREE] & CANVAS. ALL FITTINGS ARE NYLON AND, WHILE THE CHAIR IS LIGHTWEIGHT AND INCREDIBLY COMPACT, IT IS REASSURINGLY FREE FROM WOBBLE. IT'S A GOOD CHAIR TO BUY. ➡ FORM & FARVE, NIKOLAJ PLADS, COPENHAGEN,

A FOLDING CHAIR & TUBING & CANVAS FOR ABOUT $30.—
[A LEATHER VERSION, WHICH HELPS ONE SLIDE & SLIP OUT IS AVAILABLE for THE ELITE for A GOOD DEAL MORE].
DESIGNED BY ERIK MAGNUSON
AVAILABLE FROM
➡ FORM & FARVE NIKOLAJ PLADS, COPENHAGEN

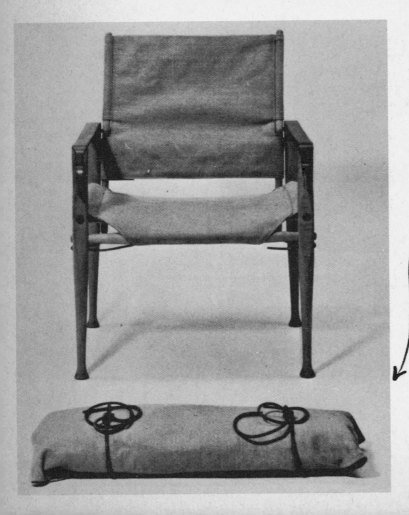

"SAFARI CHAIR"
BEECHWOOD, LINEN CANVAS & LEATHER STRAPPING.
FOLDS COMPLETELY DOWN TO ROLL. DESIGNED BY AXEL THYGESEN.
AVAILABLE FROM:

INTERNA, COPENHAGEN DENMARK

TRIPLE-BOLSTER COUCH:

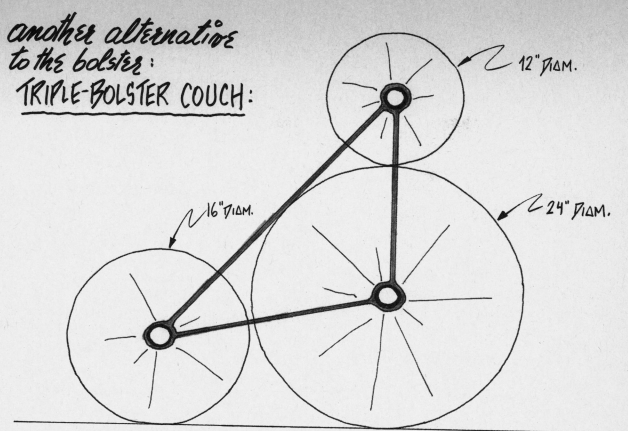

12" DIAM.

24" DIAM.

16" DIAM.

THIS COUCH CAN BE ANY WIDTH FROM 20" [FOR A SINGLE PERSON] TO ABOUT 8 FEET LONG [SEATING FOUR].

CONSTRUCTION OF THE BOLSTERS IS LIKE THE PREVIOUS CHAIR. THE STRAP AT EACH END POSITIONS THE THREE BOLSTERS AT THE MOST COMFORTABLE RELATIONSHIP. THE STRAPS CAN BE ALMOST ANY STURDY MATERIAL FROM LEATHER AND NYLON WEBBING TO ROPE OR HEAVY CLOTH.

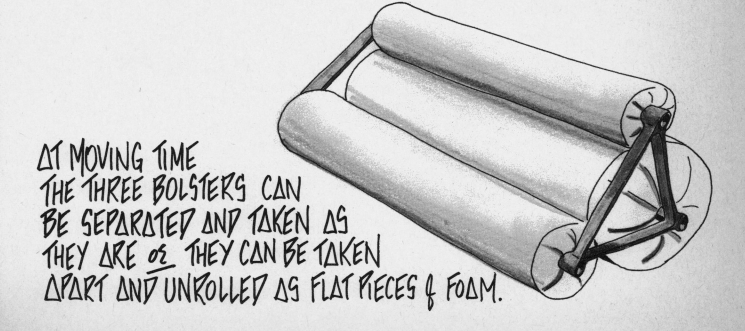

AT MOVING TIME
THE THREE BOLSTERS CAN
BE SEPARATED AND TAKEN AS
THEY ARE OR THEY CAN BE TAKEN
APART AND UNROLLED AS FLAT PIECES OF FOAM.

TWO-WAY CHAIR:

THIS MAY BE ONE of THE BEST POSSIBLE SOLUTIONS FOR A DORM or SMALL APARTMENT WHERE MULTI~PURPOSE FURNITURE IS ESSENTIAL. ◆ IT MOVES INTO 2 POSITIONS AS THE DESIGN PROVIDES FOR TWO DIFFERENT SEATING HEIGHTS: 16" FOR DINING & WORKING [THIS IS THE SAME HEIGHT AS THE "DIRECTOR'S CHAIR"] AND A 12" HEIGHT FOR RELAXING. NATURALLY, THE CHAIRS DISASSEMBLE EASILY FOR MOVING.

CONSTRUCTION IS SIMPLE: MATERIAL CAN BE 3/4" PLYWOOD or 3/4" PRESSBOARD [PICTURED ABOVE & BELOW]. ✳ PRESSBOARD WAS OUR CHOICE BECAUSE IT IS EASIER TO WORK WITH, CHEAPER, & REQUIRES LITTLE FINISHING. [PLYWOOD MIGHT HAVE TO BE "EDGED" AND PAINTED]. THE TWO SIDES WERE CUT OUT WITH A SABRE SAW, ACCORDING TO THE DIAGRAM ON THE NEXT PAGE. THESE SIDES ARE HELD TOGETHER WITH THREE 1"Ø DOWELS, EACH 20" LONG. [THE POSITIONS of THE DOWELS ARE SHOWN ON THE DIAGRAM]. FLAT-HEAD WOOD SCREWS WERE USED. ALL SLOTS ARE 1/4" WIDE AND CAN BE CUT WITH A SABRE SAW or BE ROUTED.

EACH STRIP of CANVAS HAS AN EDGE SEAM INTO WHICH A 3/8"Ø DOWEL IS SLIPPED. IT IS THESE DOWELS THAT

"LOCK" THE FABRIC SEAT-BACKS & KEEP THEM FROM SLIPPING BACK THROUGH THE SLOT. THE "FINISHED SIZE" [INCLUDING EDGE SEAMS] OF THE CANVAS SLINGS IS 14"×23".

THE FABRIC SLINGS HAVE GROMMETS ATTACHED & ARE LACED, TO KEEP THE OPENING BETWEEN THEM A CONSTANT, EVEN THOUGH THE CANVAS WILL STRETCH.

COLOURFUL PILLOWS WERE ADDED FOR MORE COMFORT & SLIGHTLY HIGHER SEATING.

*NOTE: THE PRESSBOARD VERSION WILL SAFELY SUPPORT UP TO 100 POUNDS. USE PLYWOOD FOR WEIGHTS GREATER THAN THIS.

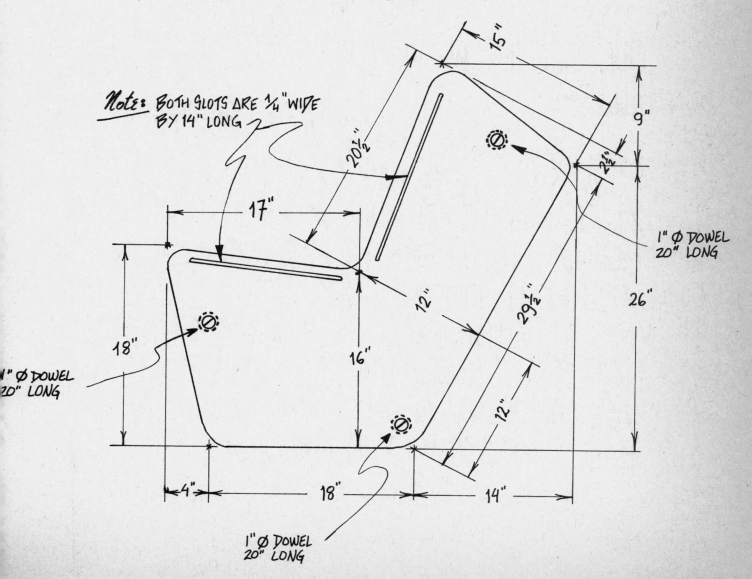

Note: BOTH SLOTS ARE 1/4" WIDE BY 14" LONG

15"
20½"
9"
2½"
17"
1" ∅ DOWEL 20" LONG
12"
29½"
26"
18"
16"
12"
1" ∅ DOWEL 20" LONG
4"
18"
14"
1" ∅ DOWEL 20" LONG

SOUND & SIGHT:

WE VALUE EXPERIENCES MORE THAN OBJECTS, FOR WE HAVE FOUND THAT POSSESSIONS ARE DISPOSABLE & FRAGILE; WHAT WE HAVE FELT, HEARD, SEEN STICKS TO THE GUT.

AND THE EXPERIENCES OF OUR SENSES WE WISH TO COMMUNICATE, TO SHARE...

ONE of VIC'S FRIENDS, A 19-YEAR OLD DANE, HAS A PASSION FOR EARLY BLACK MISSISSIPPI-DELTA BLUES SINGERS, THE SOUNDS ONLY KNOWN FROM RECORDINGS. IN TASHKENT SOMEONE ONLY KNOWN AS "ZAG" HAS A PHANTOM EXISTENCE: HE PLAYS SUPERB JAZZ BUT IS KNOWN ONLY BY HIS TAPES, WHICH ARE CIRCULATED AMONG YOUNG PEOPLE. HE HAS NEVER APPEARED IN PERSON or ON RADIO.

THESE ARE NOT EXTREME

CASES; THEY ARE PLEASANT EXAMPLES OF THE CHANGES IN PROCESSING WHAT IS "REAL".

HIGH-FIDELITY EQUIPMENT & CAMERAS TEND TO BE ENJOYED, USED, BOUGHT & TRADED EVEN BY THAT STEADILY GROWING MASS of YOUNG PEOPLE WHO ARE TURNED OFF BY OWNING THINGS, BY GADGETS AND HIGH-TECHNOLOGY STATUS OBJECTS IN GENERAL. THE REASONS ARE COMPLEX, BUT FOREMOST IS THE SHARING AND PRESERVING of EXPERIENCES.

THERE IS AN APPALLINGLY LARGE NUMBER of BOOKS, JOURNALS & MAGAZINES DEALING EXCLUSIVELY WITH HIGH-FIDELITY or PHOTOGRAPHIC EQUIPMENT. MUCH IS PUBLISHED FOR PEOPLE WHO JUST LIKE READING ABOUT NEW HARDWARE or LIKE LOOKING AT PICTURES OF MACHINES THAT TAKE PICTURES. NEW EQUIPMENT APPEARS WITH DISMAYING REGULARITY, THUS OBSOLESCING THE OLD. THE SHEER CHOICE HAS BECOME MIND-BLINDING.

IN THIS SECTION WE WANT TO SHOW JUST ONE EXAMPLE of EACH of THE CATEGORIES THAT SEEM IM- PORTANT TO US. THESE ARE NOT ENDORSEMENTS. THEY ARE OBJECTS THAT, NOMADICALLY, MAKE SENSE.

BECAUSE SOUND EQUIPMENT COSTS SO MUCH, AND SINCE PEOPLE MOVE MORE READILY FROM CONTINENT TO CONTINENT, WE HAVE ATTEMPTED TO LIST PRIMARILY EQUIPMENT THAT CARRIES INTERNAL VOLTAGE SELECTORS FOR 110V TO 250V, 50 TO 60 Hz OPERATION WITHOUT NEED FOR CONVERSION.

Note: MOST BATTERY-DRIVEN TAPE RECORDERS WITH RE-CHARGEABLE NICKEL-CADMIUM BATTERY PACKS, CAN WORK FROM 220V POWER MAINS [IN EUROPE] BY USING AN INEXPENSIVE STEP-DOWN PLUG. [SEE PAGE 138].

Note: QUADRAPHONIC SOUND IS A <u>REAL</u> TRIP! IT SOUNDS MORE THAN TWICE AS GOOD AS STEREO. HOWEVER, AT THIS TIME [AUGUST 1973] THE AVAILABLE UNITS IN JAPAN, GERMANY & THE U.S. ARE SUCH A RATS' NEST OF MATRIX EQUALIZERS, RECORD ENCODERS, 4-CHANNEL SIMULATORS, ETC., THAT NO SINGLE DECENT 110/220 V, 50/60 Hz UNIT EXISTS AS YET. HOWEVER, THERE IS AN INCREDIBLE AMOUNT OF MANUFACTURERS' INFORMATION.

PHOTOGRAPHY IS EVEN MORE COMPLEX & WE COULD FILL THIS BOOK JUST WITH DISCUSSIONS OF FILM SIZES, SQUARE VS. "IDEAL" FORMAT, ZONE SYSTEMS & THROUGH-THE-LENS METERS & MUCH ELSE. ONE FACT REMAINS: NOTHING WE SAY HERE WILL CHANGE THE FIRMLY ENTRENCHED PREJUDICES OF ANY READER WHO HAS $6000— INVESTED IN A MINOLTA SYSTEM OR LUGS A WOODEN 9×12 CAMERA ATOP HIS STATION WAGON TO BIG SUR OR THE GROSSGLOCKNER.

BUT A SECOND MAJOR FACT EMERGES AS WELL: BOTH JIM & VIC KNOW A NUMBER OF PEOPLE WITH 3 OR MORE CAMERAS ENSHRINED LIKE CROWN JEWELS IN A COMPARTMENTED CASE THAT NEVER LEAVES THE HOUSE. AND NEITHER DO CAMERAS OR LENSES...

WE'LL COMMENT ON THE IMPACT OF THE YEAR-OLD 110 FORMAT & THE "POCKET INSTA-MATICS" BY KODAK & OTHERS, IN RELATION TO NOMADICS.

WHAT TO DO ABOUT A DARKROOM WHEN THERE IS INSUFFICIENT SPACE IS SOME-THING JIM HAS THOUGHT ABOUT A LOT, SINCE HIS WIFE IS A SERIOUS PHOTOGRAPHER.

Finally: BOTH IN HIGH FIDELITY & PHOTOGRAPHY, PLEASE BE REASONABLE ABOUT WHAT YOU BUY! WE CAN'T AFFORD EVEN MORE PRODUCT POLLUTION & WASTEMAKING. IS THE SOUND SYSTEM YOU PLAN ON BUYING TOO POWERFUL FOR YOUR APARTMENT? IS THAT $980.- CAMERA REALLY THAT MUCH BETTER THAN ITS $139.- EQUIVALENT FROM EAST GERMANY? [REMEMBER: THE GREAT PHOTOS OF YESTERDAY WERE TAKEN WITH CAMERAS PRIMITIVE COMPARED TO BOTH]. HOW OFTEN WILL YOU USE THAT $495.- FISHEYE LENS? ARE YOUR EARS GOOD ENOUGH FOR THAT 600-WATT AMPLIFIER? FIRST THINK, THEN BUY IF YOU MUST.

WE'LL START WITH SIMPLES, THOUGH THE SONY TC-55 "CASSETTE-CORDER" IS A PRETTY SOPHISTICATED TOOL.

THAT'S WHAT IT IS, OF COURSE: A TOOL FOR DICTATION & NOTE-TAKING.

VIC HAS USED ONE IN EUROPE & THE U.S. FOR NEARLY ONE AND A HALF YEARS of EXTREMELY HEAVY USAGE, AND NO TROUBLE. [WHILE IN EUROPE, A STEP-DOWN PLUG IS FINE WITH THE A.C. POWER CORD FOR RECHARGING THE NICAD BATTERIES].

THE TC-55 IS THE SMALLEST UNIT [AUGUST 1973] USING STANDARD-SIZE CASSETTES. IT HAS A SPEECH/MUSIC SWITCH AND, WHILE THE SOUND IS FAR FROM GOOD oq MUSIC, IT IS SURPRISINGLY STRONG FOR A UNIT of THIS SIZE. IT HAS BEEN USED FOR "CANDID SHOTS" OF JAZZ REHEARSALS.

BUILT-IN CONDENSER MIKE & 2" SPEAKER. THE VARIOUS SERVO-MOTOR CONTROLLED CUE, PAUSE & STOP BUTTONS PERMIT FINE EDITING. AUTO-MATIC SHUT-OFF, VU RECORDING METER, BATTERIES, ETC.

FREQUENCY RESPONSE: 90 Hz TO 10 kHz @ 1⅞ IPS
WOW & FLUTTER: 0.35%

A GOOD WORKHORSE WITH ENOUGH SOPHISTICATION [MUSIC-SWITCH & EDITING FEATURES] TO MAKE IT A CANDID CAMERA FOR MUSIC. HALF-TRACK MONAURAL.

THE SECOND RECORDER USING STANDARD CASSETTES IS FROM GERMANY, THE UHER "COMPACT REPORT STEREO 124". IT IS A PROFESSIONAL-SOUNDING PRECISION MACHINE, QUITE COMPACT & FULLY TROPICALIZED. POWER INPUTS CAN BE: BATTERIES, RECHARGEABLE BATTERY PACKS, 12 V CAR or BOAT, 100-240 V, 50/60 Hz, ALL THROUGH BUILT-IN SWITCHES & CIRCUITS.

THE CASSETTE ENTERS THE MACHINE SIDEWAYS & IN THE PLAYBACK MODE, THE TAPE WILL AUTO-REVERSE UNTIL STOPPED. HOWEVER, AUTOMATIC SHUTOFF CAN ALSO BE SELECTED. BESIDES A BUILT-IN CONDENSER MIKE, A SUPERB DOUBLE STEREO MICROPHONE IS PART OF THE SET. THE CLEAR

& DEFINITE SEPARATION OF CHANNELS MAKES THIS ALSO A GOOD TRANSCRIPTION RECORDER FOR CONFERENCES. PLAYED THROUGH DECENT SPEAKERS IT HAS A FINE SOUND. FREQUENCY RESPONSE: 30 Hz TO 12.5 KHz WOW & FLUTTER: 0.12%

Finally: VIC FEELS IT IS A JOY TO SEE AN INSTRUMENT THAT DOESN'T LOOK AS MUSHY & GORPY AS MOST.

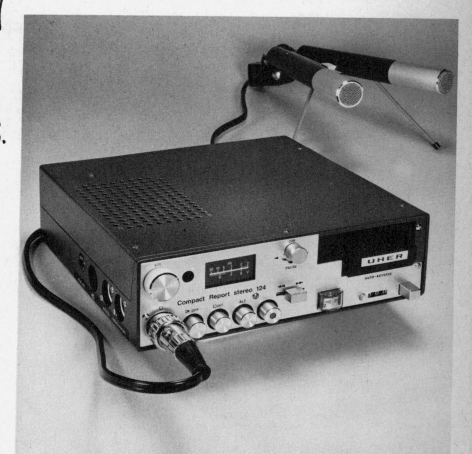

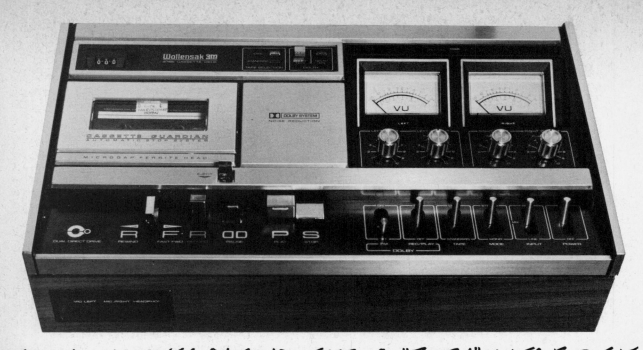

OF THE MANY CASSETTE SYSTEMS OFFERING "DOLBY" UNITS FOR THE SUPPRESSION OF TAPE-HISS, JIM FEELS THAT THIS WOLLENSAK PERFORMS EXCELLENTLY. THE TECHNICAL CHARACTERISTICS ARE GIVEN BELOW. JIM FAULTED THIS UNIT ONLY FOR A SLIGHT DIFFICULTY EXPERIENCED IN INSERTING CASSETTES. HOWEVER, THE STEEL ALIGNMENT "FINGER" THAT CAUSES THIS IS ALSO PRESENT [& GIVES THE SAME TROUBLE] IN ALL OTHER DOLBY-IZED CASSETTE UNITS WE TESTED.

IMPORTANT NOTE:

AT TIME OF WRITING, ALL DOLBY-IZED UNITS AVAILABLE IN THE U.S. ARE 120 VOLT, 60 Hz. THIS UNIT CANNOT BE USED IN EUROPE. EUROPEAN UNITS ARE 220V, 50Hz & AS OF NOW LACK INTEGRAL VOLTAGE/Hz SELECTORS!

Speed	1.875 ips
Wow and Flutter	Less than 0.15% DIN weighted.
Fast Forward and Rewind Time	45 seconds for a C-60 cassette.
Input Sensitivity	Microphone . . . 0.15 mv at 500 ohms
	Input Impedance-Line . . . 100 mv at 100 k ohms input impedance.
Output	With Output Control at maximum, 1V at OVU level.
Headphone Output	0.2 mw into 8 ohms. Adjustable output.
Distortion	Tape dependent. Distortion in electronics is typically less than 0.1% up to and beyond saturation.
Frequency Response	35-15,000 Hz ± 2db with high performance type tape.
	35-14,000 Hz ± 2db with regular tape.
Signal to Noise Ratio	Dolby System "off."
	Better than 50 db.
Noise Reduction	With Dolby System "on."
	10db @ 4,000 Hz and above.
	9db @ 2,400 Hz
	6db @ 1,200 Hz
	3db @ 600 Hz
Bias Frequency	110 KHz
Power Requirements	120 Volts AC, 60 Hz, 25 watts
End of Tape Shut Off	Fully automatic. Disengages pinch roller and heads from the cassette, reverting automatically to the "Stop" mode.
Cassette Guardian	Fully automatic. Senses a defective or stalled cassette, disengaging pinch roller and heads from the cassette, reverting automatically to the "Stop" mode.
Size	17¼" x 10¼" x 6½"
Weight	16 lbs.

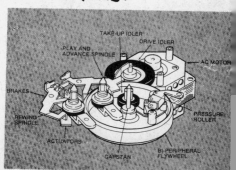

SPECIFICATIONS

The following specifications have been derived in accordance with the Institute of High Fidelity (IHF) Standard of Measurement (IHF-A-201 and IHF-T-100) in all cases where IHF standards exist. Furthermore, the amplifier power output specifications are stated in adherence to the proposed regulations of the Federal Trade Commission (FTC). The various figures, then, are **not** comparable with the loosely derived and vaguely stated specifications of many current components.

THERE ARE MANY WAYS of FITTING HI-FI COMPONENTS TOGETHER. KLH HAS MADE SOME of THE BEST & AT THE SAME TIME MOST NOMADIC MATCHED COMPONENTS for NEARLY A GENERATION NOW. FOR GOOD STEREO RE-PRODUCTION, WELL-DESIGNED & SUPERBLY CRAFTED SETS, THEIR MUSIC SYSTEMS ARE STILL REASONABLY PRICED. EVEN THOUGH DESIGNED for 120V/60Hz [U.S.] MANY YOUNG PEOPLE IN EUROPE USE KLH BUILT FOR 50 HERTZ. SOME HI-FI FREAKS ARE INTOLERANT OF THE RESTRAINED APPEARANCE of KLH; THEY WOULD PREFER A MORE "LUNA BASE III/STAR TREK" LOOK. AT ANY RATE KLH GUARANTEES ALL PARTS & LABOR FOR 2-5 YEARS! WE RECOMMEND IT HIGHLY. SHOWN IS KLH MODEL 35.

SONY DOLBY-IZED CASSETTE DECKS:

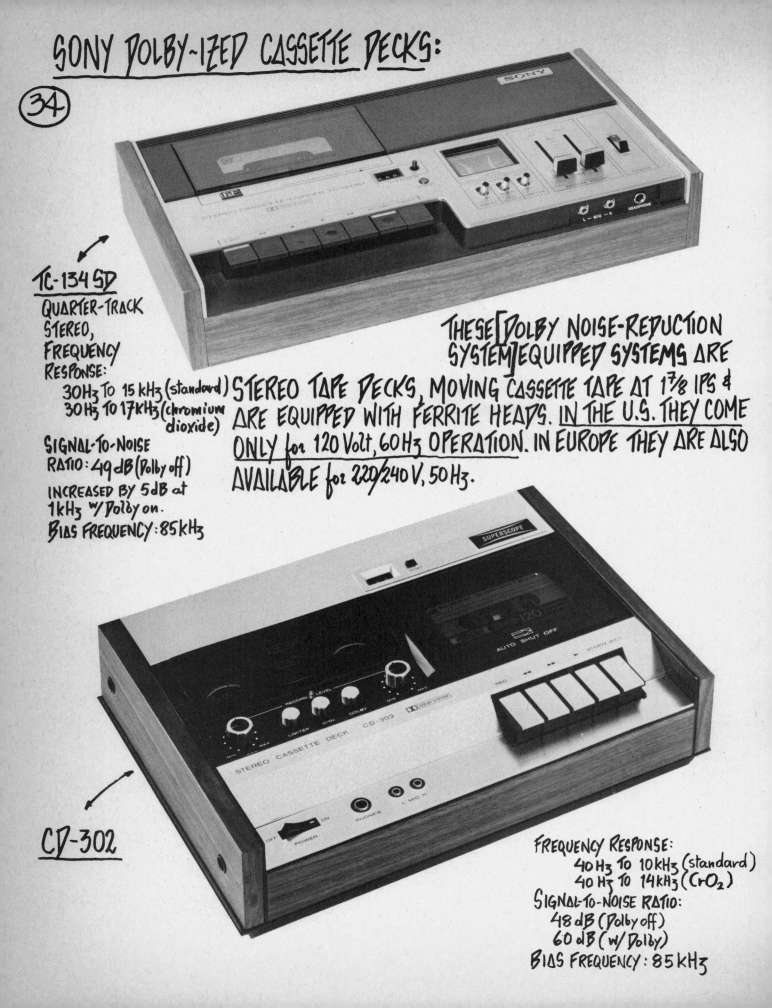

TC-134 SD

QUARTER-TRACK STEREO, FREQUENCY RESPONSE:
- 30Hz TO 15 kHz (standard)
- 30Hz TO 17kHz (chromium dioxide)

SIGNAL-TO-NOISE RATIO: 49 dB (Dolby off)

INCREASED BY 5dB at 1kHz w/ Dolby on.

BIAS FREQUENCY: 85kHz

THESE [DOLBY NOISE-REDUCTION SYSTEM] EQUIPPED SYSTEMS ARE STEREO TAPE DECKS, MOVING CASSETTE TAPE AT 1⅞ IPS & ARE EQUIPPED WITH FERRITE HEADS. IN THE U.S. THEY COME ONLY for 120 Volt, 60Hz OPERATION. IN EUROPE THEY ARE ALSO AVAILABLE for 220/240 V, 50Hz.

CD-302

FREQUENCY RESPONSE:
- 40 Hz TO 10kHz (standard)
- 40 Hz TO 14kHz (CrO_2)

SIGNAL-TO-NOISE RATIO:
- 48 dB (Dolby off)
- 60 dB (w/ Dolby)

BIAS FREQUENCY: 85 kHz

Our favorite is this

SONY TC-152 SD
SINCE IT IS ONE of THE VERY
FEW AC/DC PORTABLES WITH
DOLBY. STEREO of COURSE AND AMENABLE
(SINCE IT'S A BATTERY UNIT) TO WORLD-WIDE
USE. NOT AS RUGGED, TROPICALIZED or PRECISE
AS THE GERMAN "UHER STEREO CASSETTE REPORT", BUT IT DOES HAVE
DOLBY.

OTHER SONY STEREO UNITS THAT
ARE RELIABLE, CONVENIENT & NOT TOO
HARD ON YOUR POCKETBOOK ARE
THE TC-161SD WITH DOLBY

AND THE CF-620A SYSTEM
WITHOUT DOLBY.
BOTH of THESE SYSTEMS
HAVE FERRITE HEADS
AND [LARGELY AS A
MERCHANDISING GIMMICK]
"TOTAL-MECHANISM SHUT-OFF (TMS)" [SIC].
BOTH of THESE UNITS ARE SMALL
ENOUGH TO BE CLASSED "NOMADIC".
PERFORMANCE SPECIFICATIONS ARE
SLIGHTLY LOWER THAN THE CD-302 &
TC-134SD (PREVIOUS PAGE).

without Dolby circuits:

Tape speed: 3¾ and 7½ ips, max. deviation from nominal ± 0.2%

Wow and flutter: total rms, weighted 0.04% at 7½ ips and 0.05% at 3¾ ips. Weighted peak to peak flutter as per DIN 0.08% at 7½ ips and 0.1% at 3¾ ips

Tape slip: not exceeding 0.2%

Tape spool diameter: up to 10½ inches (minimum hub diameter 2⅜ inches)

Operating position: horizontal or vertical

Semiconductor complement: 54 transistors, 32 diodes, 4 silicon rectifiers, 1 CdS-cell

Frequency response via tape:
at 7½ ips   30 Hz to 20 kHz + 2/-3 dB
             50 Hz to 15 kHz ± 1.5 dB
at 3¾ ips   30 Hz to 16 kHz + 2/-3 dB
             50 Hz to 10 kHz ± 1.5 dB

Equalization: record NAB, playback NAB and IEC (switchable)

Distortion: measured via tape at 1 kHz peak level and at 0 VU respectively. 7½ ips less than 2% or 0.6% resp. 3¾ ips less than 3% or 1.0% resp.

Signal to noise ratio: weighted as per ASA A, readings via tape
7½ ips better than 66 dB (4-track 62 dB)
3¾ ips better than 63 dB (4-track 59 dB)

Crosstalk at 1k Hz: mono better than 60 dB, stereo better than 45 dB

Inputs per channel: Microphone, low impedance 50 to 600 ohms 0.15 mV, high impedance up to 100 k ohms 2.5 mV – Radio 2.5 mV – Auxiliary 35 mV.
All inputs have an overload margin of 40 dB (1:100)

Outputs per channel: Amplifier max. 2.5 V, internal impedance 600 ohms – Radio max. 1.2 V, internal impedance 2.5 k ohms – Headphones, volume adjustable, load impedance 200 ohms or more

with Dolby on:

All measurements taken with REVOX 601 tape, Dolby electronics switched on.

2-Track Version *(values for the 4-Track Version are shown in parenthesis)*

Signal to Noise Ratio, off tape, weighted as per CCIT:

At 7½ ips. better than 67 dB *(65 dB)*
At 3¾ ips. better than 64 dB *(62 dB)*

Weighted as per ASA A:

At 7½ ips. better than 70 dB *(67 dB)*
At 3¾ ips. better than 67 dB *(65 dB)*

Distortion measured off tape, 500 Hz Peak Level (assumed to be +6 VU)

At 7½ ips. better than 1   % *(1.5%)*
At 3¾ ips. better than 1.5 % *(2   %)*

Operating Level 0 dB (100%):

At 7½ ips. better than 0.5 % *(0.5%)*
At 3¾ ips. better than 0.5 % *(1   %)*

THIS MAY BE THE LEAST NOMADIC ITEM IN THE BOOK: BUT THE REVOX MARK III, A 77-DOLBY B STEREO RECORDER/PLAYER, IS ONE OF THE REALLY GREAT QUALITY BUILDING BLOCKS OF SOUND SYSTEMS. THERE ARE VERY FEW REEL-TO-REEL RECORDERS WITH DOLBY UNITS AVAILABLE. THE REVOX [FROM SWITZERLAND] IS A FULLY PROFESSIONAL INSTRUMENT, USED BY MANY EUROPEAN RADIO & TV NETWORKS [A 15 IPS VERSION IS AVAILABLE]. VIC HAS RECORDED CONCERTS AT 3¾ IPS, WITH EXCELLENT RESULTS, WHICH IS ALMOST UNBELIEVABLE. THE BUILT-IN OPTIONS INCLUDE: MONO, MIXING, TAPE-ON-TAPE, ECHO EFFECTS, STEREO, MULTI-PLAYBACK, AND MUCH ELSE. WE HAVE DECIDED

TO INCLUDE IT SINCE, IN ADDITION TO ITS TOP QUALITY, IT IS A REAL TRAVELLER: AUTOMATIC SWITCHING [INTERNAL] FROM 110V to 250V, 50/60 Hz.

WITH THE LARGE, STUDIO-SIZED SPOOLS, 4-TRACK & 3¾ IPS, NEARLY 15 HOURS CAN GO ON ONE TAPE; 3 HOURS 44 MINUTES WITHOUT INTERRUPTION.

HERE WE SHOW THE UNIT GANG-STACKED WITH THE MARK III A 78 AMPLIFIER & THE A 76 FM STEREO TUNER. WE FEEL THAT IT IS ABOUT THE ULTIMATE IN QUALITY AND EVEN THOUGH THE PRICE IS HEAVY, OTHER UNITS AT COMPARABLE PRICES TEND TO SPEND MORE ON STYLING & LESS ON ELECTRONICS AND QUALITY CONTROL. AVAILABLE FROM HI-FI STORES AND ➡

REVOX INTERNATIONAL
ELA AG
CH-8105 REGENSDORF-ZÜRICH
SWITZERLAND

a little about SPEAKERS:

AS WE'VE SAID BEFORE, THIS IS NO HI-FI MANUAL.
BUT THERE ARE A FEW THINGS WE THINK MAY HELP YOU CHOOSE:

- SPEAKERS ARE LIKE GOLD: GENERALLY THE MORE THEY WEIGH, THE MORE THEY'RE WORTH. A SUBSTANTIAL CABINET WILL GIVE MINIMALLY BETTER BASS RESPONSE.

- LET YOUR EARS GUIDE YOU. LISTEN TO DIFFERENT SPEAKER PAIRS & MAKE YOUR CHOICE ON THE BASIS OF HOW THEY SOUND TO YOU, RATHER THAN INVOLVED SPECIFICATIONS or CABINET STYLING.

- IDEALLY EACH CABINET SHOULD CONTAIN A THREE-WAY CROSSOVER NETWORK FEEDING A HIGH-COMPLIANCE BASS WOOFER [8"ø or LARGER], A 5" MIDRANGE AND A DOME TWEETER.

- SPEAKERS MUST BE CAPABLE of HANDLING THE OUTPUT WATTAGE & YOUR AMPLIFIER.

- MANY KITS FOR BUILDING SPEAKER CABINETS ARE AVAILABLE. THESE ARE EASY TO BUILD & WILL SAVE YOU MUCH MONEY.

- "ELECTROSTATIC" SPEAKERS PLUG INTO MAIN OUTLETS, HENCE POSE THE U.S./EUROPE 110 VOLT/220 VOLT PROBLEM.

POCKET INSTAMATIC CAMERAS:

TROUBLE IS, TOO MANY PEOPLE HAVE FIRST-RATE CAMERAS, SLOWLY AGING IN SOME CLOSET: IT'S TOO MUCH BOTHER TO PACK CAMERA, LENSES, ETC.

WHILE MINIATURE, SUB-MINIATURE & "SPY" CAMERAS HAVE BEEN AROUND FOR NEARLY 90 YEARS, KODAK APPROACHED THE PROBLEM OF CREATING A REALLY NOMADIC CAMERA AS SYSTEMS DESIGN. FILMS, PROCESSING METHODS, CAMERAS & PROJECTORS WERE DESIGNED COMPATIBLY & MARKET-READY AT THE SAME TIME. THE NEW 110 FILM SIZE, NEGATIVE 13 × 17 mm, CAN PRINT POSTCARD-SIZE, AND SLIDES CAN PROJECT WELL [EXCEPT FOR GRAIN]. THE POINT OF COURSE IS CONVENIENCE & PORTABILITY. AND PEOPLE DO TEND TO SLIP ONE OF THESE CAMERAS IN THEIR POCKET BEFORE SETTING OUT ON A TRIP & TO LEAVE BULKIER EQUIPMENT BEHIND.

BECAUSE OF GOOD SYSTEMS DESIGN, THE KODAK POCKET INSTAMATIC 60 STILL TENDS TO BE FAR BETTER THAN RECENT JAPANESE, GERMAN & U.S. COPIES.* PROCESSING PRICES ARE PROHIBITIVE, HOWEVER. MAIN DRAWBACK: FIXED LENS.

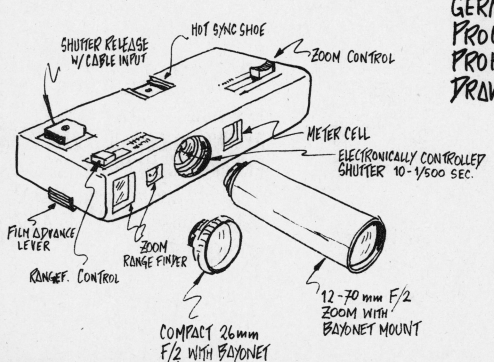

SHUTTER RELEASE W/ CABLE INPUT

HOT SYNC SHOE

ZOOM CONTROL

METER CELL

ELECTRONICALLY CONTROLLED SHUTTER 10 - 1/500 SEC.

FILM ADVANCE LEVER

ZOOM RANGE FINDER

RANGEF. CONTROL

COMPACT 26mm F/2 WITH BAYONET MOUNT

12 - 70 mm F/2 ZOOM WITH BAYONET MOUNT

"MODERN PHOTOGRAPHY" BEGAN DESIGNING A BETTER POCKET INSTAMATIC NEARLY TWO YEARS AGO. WE SHOW IT HERE, SOMEWHAT UPDATED. NOTHING LIKE IT EXISTS SO FAR.

* AN AMAZING TRIBUTE TO GOOD SYSTEMS DESIGN IN A FAST-CHANGING AREA LIKE PHOTOGRAPHY & AFTER 2 YEARS!

FOLDING, ROLLING, TUCK-AWAY DARKROOM:

JIM DESIGNED THIS FOR HIS OWN & SARA'S USE ➡ IT CONVERTS THEIR BATHROOM INTO A PHOTO LAB.

THE TOTAL WIDTH OF THE UNIT IS ONLY 23½" (WHEN FOLDED). IF IT WERE WIDER IT WOULD NOT GO THROUGH BATHROOM DOORS.

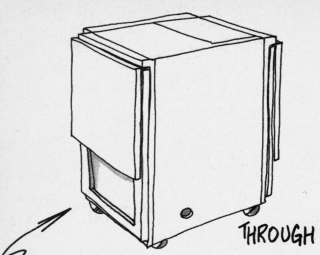

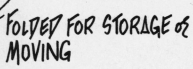

FOLDED FOR STORAGE OR MOVING

IMPORTANT NOTE:

THIS SYSTEM WAS DESIGNED AROUND AN OMEGA B-22 ENLARGER. MEASURE YOUR OWN ENLARGER AND CHANGE DESIGN DIMENSIONS AS AND IF NEEDED.

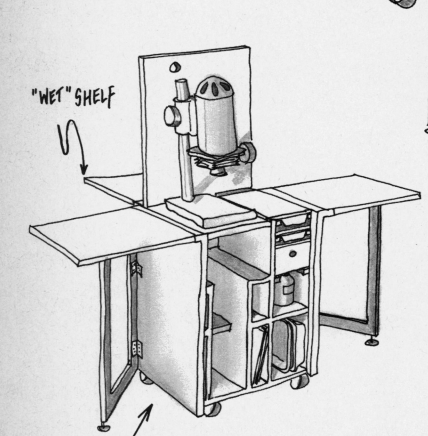

"WET" SHELF

COMPLETE DARKROOM OPERATIONAL

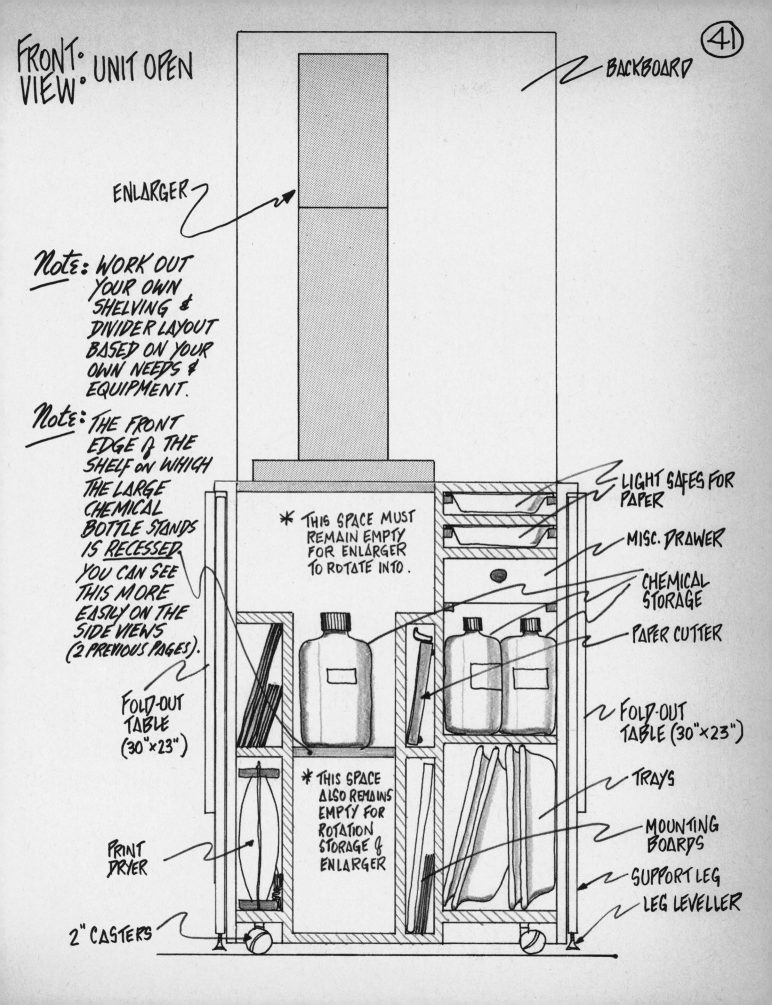

FRONT: UNIT OPEN
VIEW:

BACKBOARD

ENLARGER

Note: WORK OUT YOUR OWN SHELVING & DIVIDER LAYOUT BASED ON YOUR OWN NEEDS & EQUIPMENT.

Note: THE FRONT EDGE OF THE SHELF ON WHICH THE LARGE CHEMICAL BOTTLE STANDS IS RECESSED. YOU CAN SEE THIS MORE EASILY ON THE SIDE VIEWS (2 PREVIOUS PAGES).

* THIS SPACE MUST REMAIN EMPTY FOR ENLARGER TO ROTATE INTO.

LIGHT SAFES FOR PAPER

MISC. DRAWER

CHEMICAL STORAGE

PAPER CUTTER

FOLD-OUT TABLE (30"×23")

FOLD-OUT TABLE (30"×23")

* THIS SPACE ALSO REMAINS EMPTY FOR ROTATION STORAGE & ENLARGER

TRAYS

MOUNTING BOARDS

PRINT DRYER

SUPPORT LEG

LEG LEVELLER

2" CASTERS

Working information:

- THE WHOLE SYSTEM HAS BEEN DESIGNED FOR 3/4" PLYWOOD OR FINNPLY.
- THE DRAWINGS ON THIS & THE NEXT TWO PAGES ARE SCALED 1/8"=1". SO TAKE THE MEASUREMENTS RIGHT off THESE PAGES ➡ WE DIDN'T WANT TO CONFUSE YOU WITH TOO MANY DIMENSIONS & DIMENSION LINES ➡ ESPECIALLY AS YOU WILL CHANGE SOME SIZES TO FIT YOUR OWN ENLARGER, RATHER THAN JIM'S OMEGA B-22.
- CAREFULLY INSPECT YOUR OWN ENLARGER TO SEE IF ANY PARTS or LENSES WILL FALL OFF WHEN THE ENLARGER IS INVERTED. IF SO, MAKE PROVISIONS FOR AFFIXING THEM, PADDING THEM or REMOVING THEM BEFORE PUTTING THE UNIT IN STORAGE POSITION ➡ THE CONDENSER SYSTEM LENSES ARE ESPECIALLY DAMAGE~PRONE.
- REMEMBER AGAIN: WHEN FOLDED, TOTAL WIDTH, INCLUDING REAR FOLD-OUT "WET" SHELF & SUPPORT LEG, IS 23½", TO GO THROUGH BATHROOM DOORS.
- 2" BALL CASTERS ARE RECESSED UP INTO THE BOTTOM TO KEEP UNIT LOW. ALLOW 4" BOX FOR CASTERS TO ROTATE.

PIVOT POINT

10"×12" STORAGE SHELF

ENLARGER

SIDE·UNIT IN CLOSED POSITION VIEW·

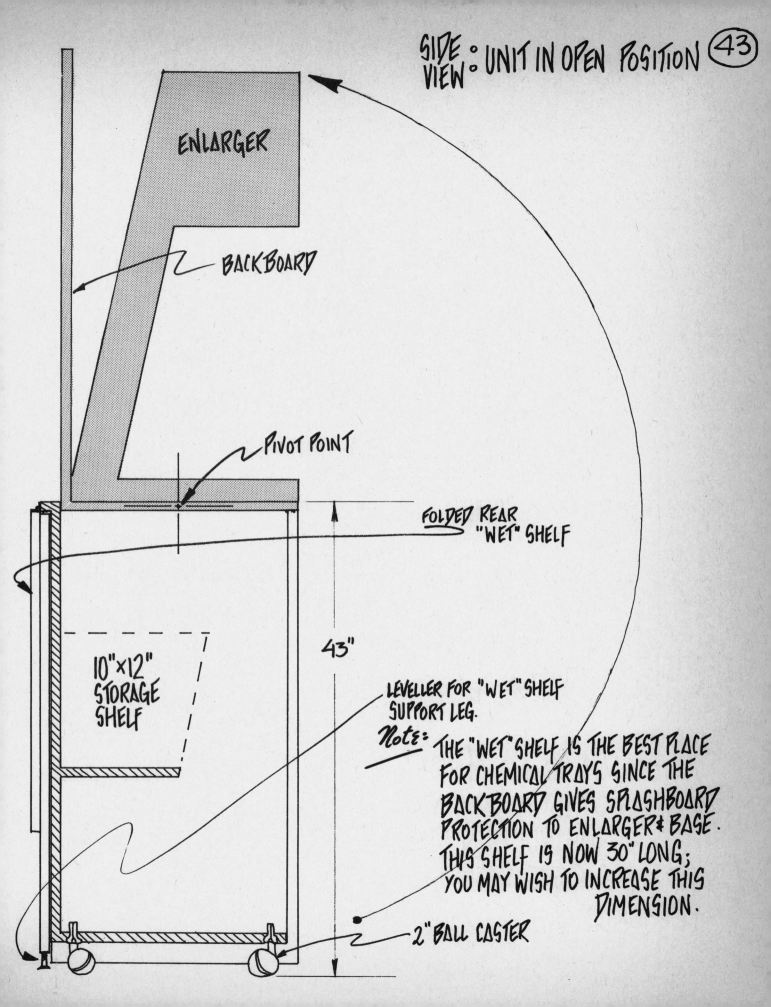

ENLARGER

BACKBOARD

PIVOT POINT

FOLDED REAR "WET" SHELF

43"

10"×12" STORAGE SHELF

LEVELLER FOR "WET" SHELF SUPPORT LEG.

Note: THE "WET" SHELF IS THE BEST PLACE FOR CHEMICAL TRAYS SINCE THE BACKBOARD GIVES SPLASHBOARD PROTECTION TO ENLARGER & BASE. THIS SHELF IS NOW 30" LONG; YOU MAY WISH TO INCREASE THIS DIMENSION.

2" BALL CASTER

lighting: ㊹

WE STILL STRONGLY FEEL THAT LIGHTING CAN BE CLASSIFIED IN FOUR WAYS:

a/ DIRECT LIGHTING ➡ CONCENTRATED WORK LIGHT
b/ INDIRECT LIGHTING ➡ DIFFUSED, "MOOD" LIGHT
c/ ORNAMENTAL LIGHTING ➡ THE LIGHT SOURCE ITSELF BECOMES IMPORTANT
d/ A COMBINATION OF THESE

THERE ARE PROBABLY FAR TOO MANY LIGHTS & LAMPS IN EXISTENCE, MANY OF THEM NOMADIC. IN THE FOLLOWING PAGES WE HAVE TRIED TO SHOW YOU WHAT IS AVAILABLE & WHAT YOU CAN MAKE YOURSELF.

SINCE MANY OTHERWISE INTELLIGENT PEOPLE MANAGE TO ELECTROCUTE THEMSELVES WHILE TRYING TO DO SIMPLE WIRING, JIM HAS WRITTEN A BRIEF INSTRUCTION MANUAL ON WIRING, WHICH WE INCLUDE. REMEMBER THAT WHAT WE HAVE SAID APPLIES PRIMARILY TO THE U.S.A., CANADA & JAPAN, ONLY IN

PART TO EUROPE, AFRICA & ASIA. ENGLAND, UNABLE TO ENFORCE EVEN THE SIMPLEST STANDARDIZATION LAWS, IS NOT INCLUDED BECAUSE OF THE DIVERSITY OF PLUGS, OUTLETS, WIRING, BAYONET-MOUNTED BULBS [SHADES OF 1896, HONESTLY!], ETC.

JAN TRÄGÅRDH OF COPENHAGEN, A LEADING INDUSTRIAL DESIGNER, HAS A SUGGESTION ABOUT HALF-SILVERED BULBS. WHILE THESE BULBS ARE INCREASING IN POPULARITY, THEY ARE VERY EXPENSIVE & IN SOME PLACES HARD TO GET. JAN'S ANSWER: DO IT YOURSELF.

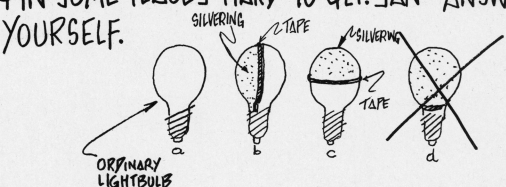

TAPE HALF THE BULB WITH DRAFTSMAN'S MASKING TAPE, SPRAY WITH CHROMIUM OR ALUMINUM SPRAY PAINT. WHEN DRY, REMOVE THE TAPE. *caution:* IN CASE "b" ABOVE, MAKE A MARK ON THE SIDE OF THE THREADING SO THAT WHEN RE-INSERTING THE BULB IN THE LAMP, THE REFLECTING SURFACE FACES AS YOU WANTED IT. IN CASE "d": DON'T! NEVER COVER MORE THAN 50% OF THE BULB SURFACE, ELSE THE FILAMENTS WILL MELT.

HOW TO WIRE AND HANG A LAMP WITHOUT ELECTROCUTING YOURSELF

In this short education course, we will primarily discuss suspended or hanging lamps, as these are often the most difficult to locate, wire and suspend. Lesson 3, *Wiring Up a Lamp Socket,* is, of course, universal for all types of lamps.

LESSON 1.   THE LOCATION
Once you have determined exactly where, according to your lighting needs, you want to hang the lamp, the next step is to locate the power source. The source will probably be one of three possibilities: the *Ceiling Cap-plate,* the *Ceiling Outlet or Socket* and the *Wall Outlet.*

LESSON 2.   THE CEILING CAP-PLATE
This is not only the most difficult to wire up but possibly the most dangerous. Always exercise extreme caution around anything electrical. Check and double-check each step and always be suspicious of any and all wiring.

STEP 1.   It is necessary to cut power to the ceiling cap-plate box before you do anything, including removing the coverplate. The simplest way is to screw a lightbulb into the present fixture and turn it on. Then, locate your household fusebox and begin removing each fuse (or turning off each switch) in turn until you find the one that controls the lightbulb. When you have located the correct fuse, remove it (turn the switch to OFF) until you are completely finished with the wiring. This step is *mandatory.* You must be assured that the circuit on which you are working is DEAD.

STEP 2.   Remove the screws from the cap-plate and lower it slowly to expose the wiring. If a hanging lamp is already attached to the cap-plate, have an assistant hold the lamp so that it does not put stress on the wires. Never let a heavy lamp dangle from the wiring.

STEP 3.   Visually inspect the ceiling box wiring. Don't stick your fingers in there yet! There may be more wires than you need to fool with (or care to). You will see that the lamp wires are attached to the house wiring with colourful screw-on plastic caps. There will usually be two wires coming from the lamp. Often these wires are colour-coded but sometimes they are not. The house wiring onto which these wires are attached usually displays the colour-codes of black and white. White is the "ground" side of the line voltage while black is the "hot" side. One of the leads from the lamp should go to one or more black wires and the other lamp lead should go to one or more white wires. In addition, some lamps have a third, green wire which is a mechanical "ground" wire and should be located under a screw on the outlet box and not connected to a wire. If there are other wires connected to the black and white leads in addition to the lamp wires, see to it that they are connected exactly as you found them after wiring in your lamp. If you should find both RED and black and white wires in the box, it is an indication that there is more than one circuit present and the second may still be HOT! Go back to your fusebox and, if necessary, cut power to the whole house. In this case, it's better to be healthy, safe and alive than to worry about the ice cubes melting or having to reset the clocks.

STEP 4.   Once you have carefully surveyed the wiring and have satisfied yourself that it is safe, you may locate the two lamp wires and remove the screw-on plastic caps that connect them. Again, one of the lamp leads should go to a single or group of white wires while the other lamp lead should go to a single or group of black (red) wires. You must always approach these wires with extreme caution. If possible, try to do most of your work with one hand, as this has often prevented electrical shock by limiting how many wires you can touch simultaneously. Once you have twisted off the plastic caps and removed the old lamp wires, you wrap on the new leads after threading them through the cap-plate as the old wires were. Now thread the plastic caps back onto each wire.

STEP 5.   Recheck the box. Make sure all the plastic caps are on and secure. They must be on tightly so that no bare wires show around the junction. See to it that the wiring is neat, orderly and uncramped. Make sure everything is wired as you first found it. One lamp lead must go to white, the other to red or black. Any green wires should be screwed to the box. Now check everything again! When you have satisfied yourself that everything is correct, carefully store the wiring up into the box and screw the cap-plate cover on tightly.

STEP 6.   You should now have a correctly wired lamp cord hanging from your ceiling. The last step is to attach a lamp socket as per lesson 3 which follows. You may not reconnect the fuse until the socket is attached to the end of the lamp cord. Once this is accomplished, reconnect the fuse at the fusebox. If the fuse does not blow out (or the switch trip) and the light lights, you can feel proud of the fact that you have now accomplished what a professional electrician would have charged a goodly sum for. If, however, the bulb does not light or the fuse blows, retrace each step carefully and get advice!

LESSON 3.   WIRING UP A LAMP SOCKET

The illustration on page 49 shows a typical lamp socket. The particular socket shown is designed to be attached by a threaded tube coupler; however, it works equally well for hanging lamps. The socket consists of three major parts: the metal cap, the metal barrel and the plastic receptacle insert. To wire the socket, first determine at what height you want the bulb to hang. (Remember, power to the circuit is still OFF.) Cut the cord slightly above this mark and strip about ½" of insulation from each wire. Twist the bare strands with your fingertips to keep them from fraying. Now, run the lamp cord through the hole in the cap (note illustration) and slide the cap up the cord and out of the way while you wire the receptacle. Take each wire separately and bend the bare, twisted wire into a U shape. Screw one wire under the screw on one side of the receptacle, then screw the other wire under the other screw. Trim the excess wire right at the screw. Remove the cardboard collar from the barrel and slide it onto the plastic receptacle so that it covers the screws and the wire-ends. Then slide the metal barrel over the collar. The barrel and the metal cap then press-fit together with a "click." Make sure no wiring shorts out to the metal barrel or cap. If you follow the illustration, you should have no difficulties. That's all there is to it!

LESSON 4.   THE CEILING OUTLET or SOCKET

In this case you already have a socket on the ceiling. Actually, this is much more likely than Lesson 2. Undoubtedly there is a gorpy-looking glass "shade" hiding a perfectly good outlet with a bulb in it. All that is required is to remove the glass canopy in order to use the already-present outlet. No wiring at the ceiling will be required because there is an adaptor that neatly screws into the bulb socket and becomes a standard plug outlet. (See Illustration A, next page.) All you need to do now is attach a regular appliance plug onto the lamp cord and plug it in! By following Lesson 3, you can attach the lamp socket (UNPLUG IT FIRST) and you're in business. Sometimes you have a relatively heavy lamp that keeps unplugging itself. Try slightly bending the prongs of the plugs to make it fit tighter. If that doesn't work, you will have to tether the lamp from an anchor or eye-bolt in the ceiling.

LESSON 5.   THE WALL OUTLET

This is actually the easiest way, but slightly more costly, as you have to buy a long lamp cord. Simply enough, the lamp hangs from an anchor or eye-bolt screwed into the ceiling. The cord runs up from the lamp, through the eye-bolt and across the ceiling to the wall. There, you must put another eye-bolt to support the cord as it runs down the wall to the outlet. You may even be able to find a quick-mount plug which has the cord coming out at a right angle, thus keeping it close to the wall. By allowing some extra cord and the means to adjust it, you can raise or lower the lamp, a nice idea for rooms that must serve more than one purpose.

LESSON 6.   NEVER TRUST ANYONE

Since we cannot and will not be held responsible if you melt your lamp, blow up your house or electrocute yourself, you should plan to take great pains to learn a little more about electricity than is presented here. SEARS has a good little house-wiring booklet, as do many other large stores, bookstores and electrical outlets. You may find them interesting. Lastly, never trust anyone when it concerns YOUR life. Don't rely completely on Vic or Jim, a friend or even *yourself.* If you don't understand any of the previous instructions or are confused about them, get assistance from someone qualified!!! Don't blunder on by yourself. Very often the guy at the electrical store will be glad to answer your questions without charging you, and don't be afraid to telephone someone and hassle them for an answer. Good people won't mind taking the time.

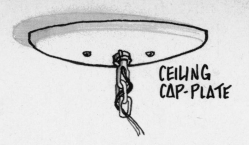

CEILING
CAP-PLATE

CEILING
OUTLET

LAMP
SOCKET:

CAP

RECEPTACLE

CARDBOARD
SLEEVE

BARREL

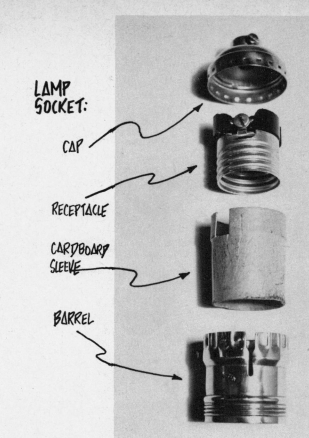

Ⓐ SCREW-IN TO
PLUG-IN ADAPTOR

WALL OUTLET

Ⓒ CUBE "TAP"

Ⓓ CORD
SWITCH

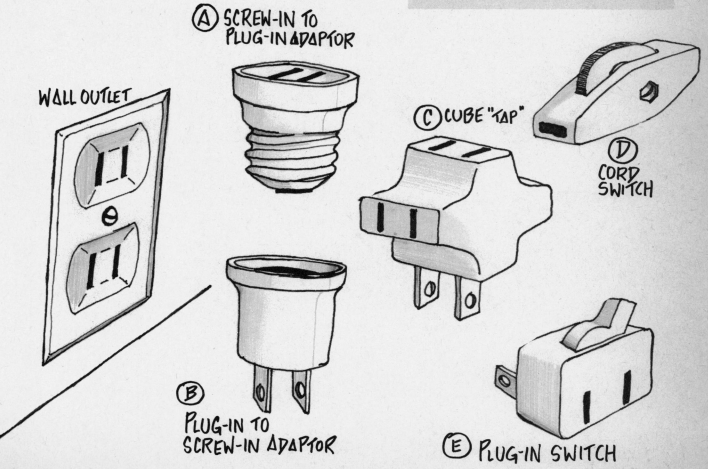

Ⓑ PLUG-IN TO
SCREW-IN ADAPTOR

Ⓔ PLUG-IN SWITCH

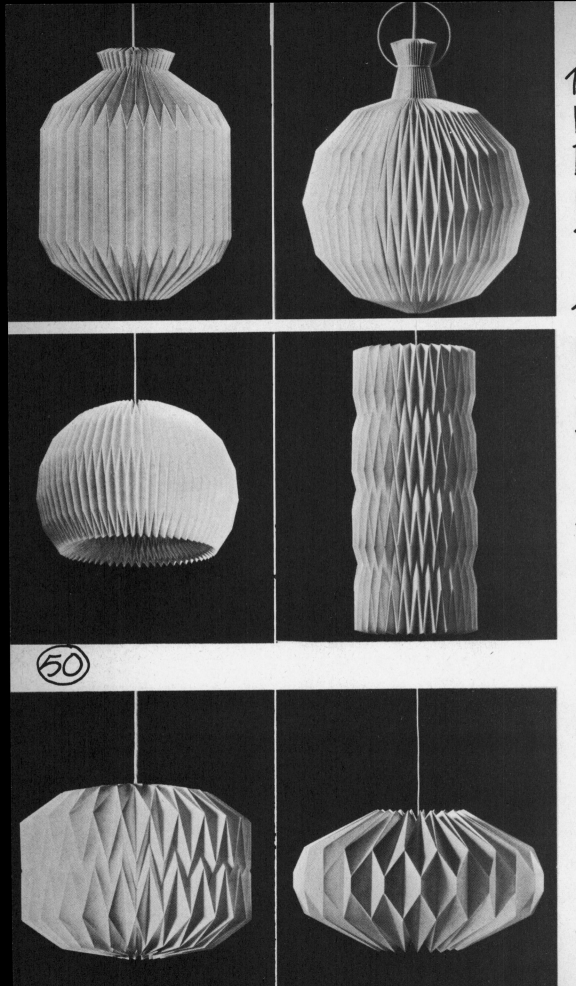

(50)

THE DANISH FIRM LE KLINT HAS DESIGNED & MADE LAMPSHADES LIKE THESE FOR MORE THAN 60 YEARS.

THEY ARE MADE OF PAPER THAT IS PLASTICIZED & OF SHEET PLASTIC BY SCORING & FOLDING.

THEY ARE LIGHT~WEIGHT & SINCE THEY FOLD, AS NOMADIC AS CAN BE.

SOME HAVE BEEN IN CONTINUOUS USE FOR 30 YEARS WITHOUT ANY SIGNIFICANT DISCOLOURATION.

THE 12 LAMPS

ON THESE TWO PAGES ARE ONLY SHOWN AS REPRESENTING NEARLY 100 MORE.

YOU'LL SEE THAT THEIR LINE INCLUDES ALSO CEILING FIXTURES & STANDING LAMPS. ALL OF THESE COME IN MANY SIZES & ARE NOT EXPENSIVE. IN OUR EARLIER BOOK (page 133) WE'VE ALSO SUGGESTED THAT YOU CAN TRY FOLDING.

➤ LE KLINT
EGGESTUBBEN 13-15
5270 NÆSBY
DENMARK
SHOWROOM:
ST. KIRKESTRÆDE 1
COPENHAGEN

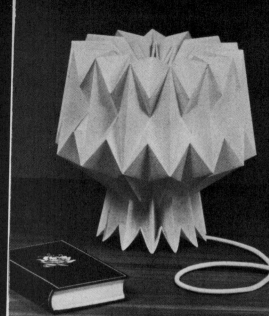

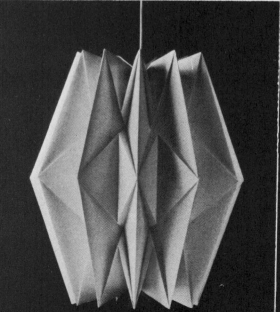

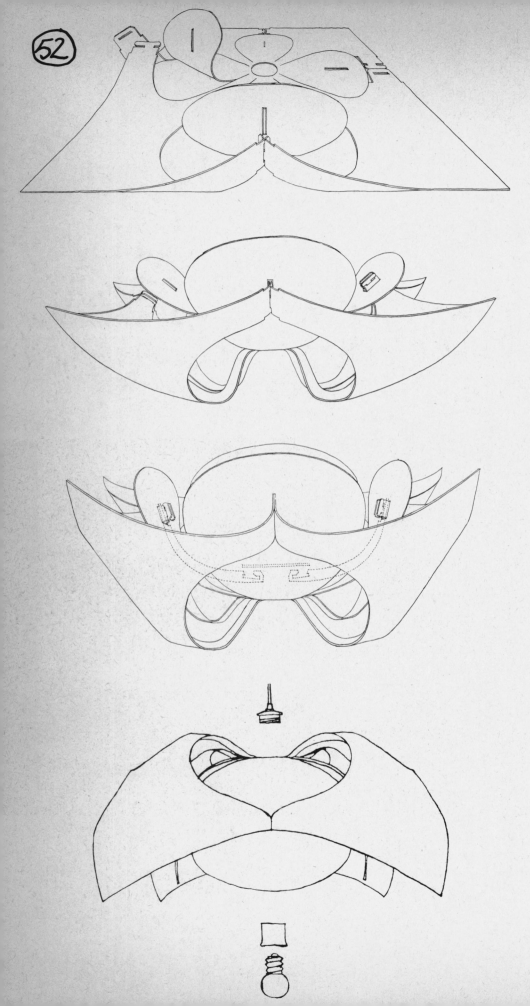

STILL FROM
LE KLINT:

"JOKER"

THIS ASSEMBLE-IT-
YOURSELF LAMP-
SHADE IS MADE
OF THIN SHEET
PLASTIC AND
COMES IN SEVEN
SEMI-TRANSLUCENT
COLOURS, AND
THREE SIZES.

AS YOU
CAN SEE, IT
FOLDS BACK
DOWN TO A
FLAT SHEET.

IN A WAY, "JOKER" IS TYPICAL of ALL THAT IS BEST IN SIMPLE & SUB~ DUED DANISH LAMP DESIGN.

THE DESIGNER IS CHRISTIAN RÆDER, A PART-TIME STUDENT OF VIC'S AT THE ROYAL DANISH ACADEMY.

LE KLINT HAS OTHER PLASTIC SHEET LAMPS, BUT ON THESE

LAST FOUR PAGES WE HAVE ONLY SHOWN THOSE THAT REALLY FOLD UP or "UNBUTTON" TO BE NOMADIC.

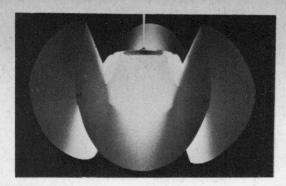

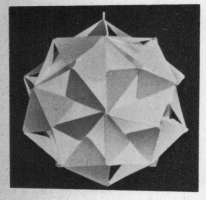

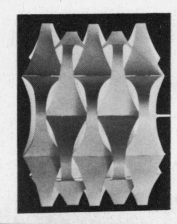

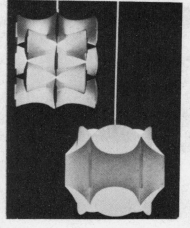

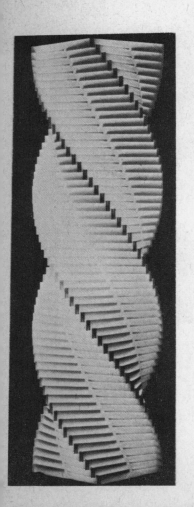

THESE LAMPS ARE ONLY A FEW EXAMPLES OF LITERALLY DOZENS THAT ARE AVAILABLE IN 10 DIFFERENT COLOURS, METALLIC FINISHES, ETC.

ALL OF THEM CONSIST OF MANY PLASTIC PIECES THAT "BUTTON" TOGETHER IN 30 MINUTES OR LESS.

PRICES START AT LESS THAN $2.– BUT CAN GO AS HIGH AS $40.–.

THEY COME IN A FLAT PACKAGE [LIKE AN L.P. RECORD] & CAN BEST BE ORDERED FROM A DEPARTMENT STORE IN COPENHAGEN:

➡ ILLUM, 52 ØSTERGADE, COPENHAGEN or MAGASIN du NORD, KONGENS NYTORV, COPENHAGEN.

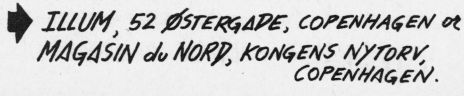

POUL HENNINGSEN DID A GREAT DEAL OF RESEARCH ABOUT AN ELLIPSOIDAL SHAPE FOR IDEAL WORKING LIGHTS.

THE RESULT IS A LAMP THAT NOT ONLY GIVES OPTIMAL LIGHT AT THE IMMEDIATE WORK SURFACE, BUT ALSO LIGHTS UP REMOTE CORNERS OF DRAWING TABLE OR DESK, PREVENTING CONTRAST~DAZZLE.

IT COMES WITH A 3-WAY SWITCH, TWO DIFFERENT-LENGTH "LUXO"-TYPE ARMS, AND EXISTS IN WHITE, BLACK OR CHROME. AVAILABLE FROM SHOPS AND:

➡ LOUIS POULSEN & CO., NYHAVN 11, COPENHAGEN

(55)

56

"PARENTESI" IS THE NAME OF THIS INCREDIBLY NOMADIC LAMP. IT WAS DESIGNED BY THE ARCHITECT ACHILLE CASTIGLIONI FROM AN IDEA BY PIO MANZÙ. A STEEL CABLE IS HELD TAUT BY A LEAD WEIGHT COVERED WITH BLACK RUBBER. THE STEEL "PARENTHESIS", WITH THE REFLECTOR BULB IN A UNIVERSAL JOINT, SLIDES EASILY UP or DOWN & STAYS IN PLACE BECAUSE OF ITS OWN FRICTION.

A VERY STEEP PRICE MAKES IT ELITIST, BUT ITS SUPERB LOGIC KEEPS IT FROM BEING TRIVIAL.

EVERYTHING BUT THE BULB COMES IN A NEAT PACKAGE. →

AVAILABLE FROM:

➥ FLOS
VIA MORETTO 58,
25100 BRESCIA
ITALY

ATELIER INTERNTL.
139 E. 57 ST.
NEW YORK, N.Y
U.S.A.

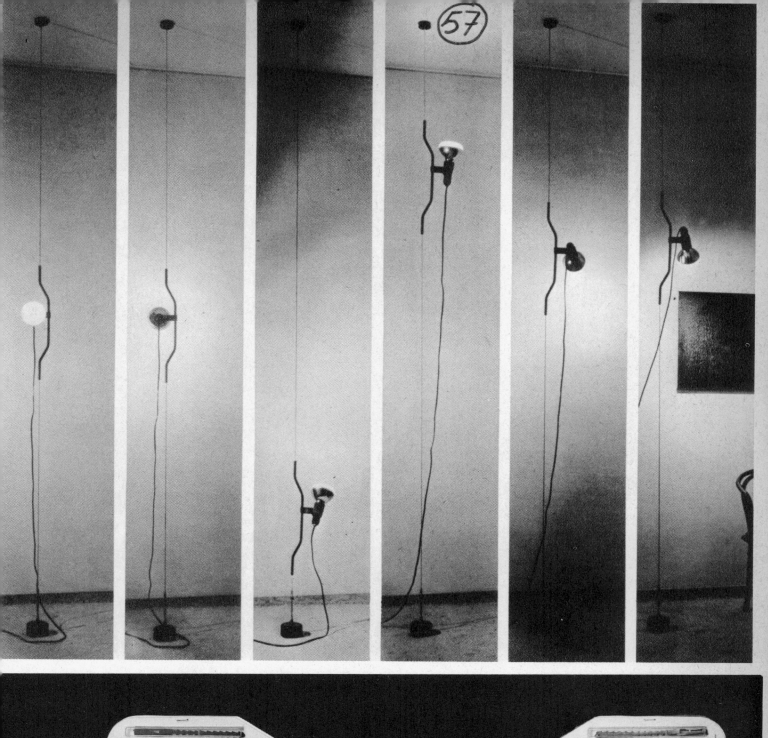
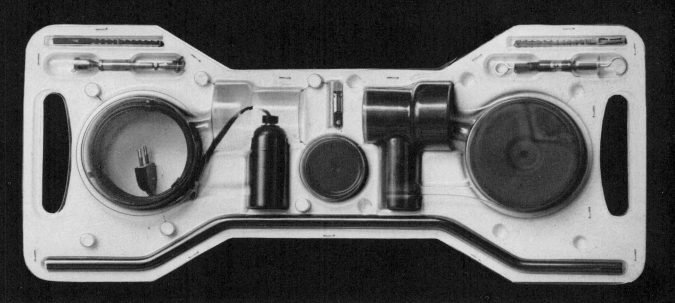

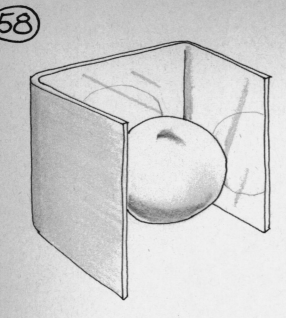

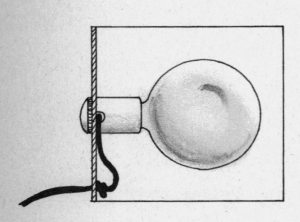

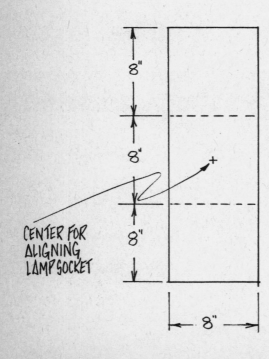

CENTER FOR
ALIGNING
LAMP SOCKET

8"
8"
8"
8"

SIMPLE GLOBE LAMP:

UNUSUALLY SIMPLE TO BUILD. YOU MAY USE EITHER SHEET METAL OR HEAVY CARDBOARD.

➤ IF YOU USE CARDBOARD, GLUE ALUMINUM FOIL TO ONE SIDE BEFORE BENDING. (WORK ALL THE BUBBLES OUT!) THE ALUMINUM IS ESSENTIAL, BOTH AS A LIGHT REFLECTOR & TO DISSIPATE HEAT. AFTER BENDING, COVER THE EXTERIOR WITH COLOURED PAPER.
USE A "QUICK-MOUNT" TYPE SOCKET (SHOWN TO THE LEFT) SINCE THIS AUTOMATICALLY MAKES CONNECTION TO THE WIRES AS YOU TIGHTEN THE REAR CAP.

➤ THE SHEET-METAL VERSION IS EVEN EASIER TO MAKE, IF YOU HAVE ACCESS TO METAL SHEARS & A DRILL.
LEAVE THE METAL INSIDE BARE, BUT PAINT THE EXTERIOR IF YOU WISH.
BE SURE SMOOTH EDGES EXIST BY FILING EDGES & CORNERS DOWN. USE A SCREW-DOWN LAMP SOCKET & MAKE SURE THE WIRING DOES NOT TOUCH THE SHEET METAL.
LAST, PUT A "STRAIN-RELIEF" KNOT IN THE CORD & RUN IT THROUGH A HOLE IN THE REAR. MOUNT A SWITCH & PLUG TO THE CORD.
USE A GLOBE BULB.
THIS UNIT [OR SEVERAL] CAN STAND ON A TABLE OR DESK OR BE WALL-MOUNTED.

ADJUSTABLE LAMP:

HERE'S ANOTHER CARDBOARD LAMP:

SCRIBE THE PATTERN ONTO A PIECE OF RIGID BUT BENDABLE CARDBOARD. LINE ONE SIDE WITH ALUMINUM FOIL [SPRAY ADHESIVE WORKS WELL — WORK OUT THE AIR BUBBLES!] FOLD SO THAT THE FOIL IS INSIDE. NOW LOCK THE LAMP TOGETHER WITH 3 ENVELOPE FASTENERS. BE SURE TO INCLUDE THE REAR PANEL TAB. USE A "QUICK-MOUNT" TYPE SOCKET AND INSTALL IT IN THE CENTER OF REAR PANEL.

Note: BULB MUST BE 60 WATTS OR LESS!

BEND SUPPORT FORK & FIX w/ 2 WOODEN DRAWER KNOBS [DETAIL BELOW, RIGHT].

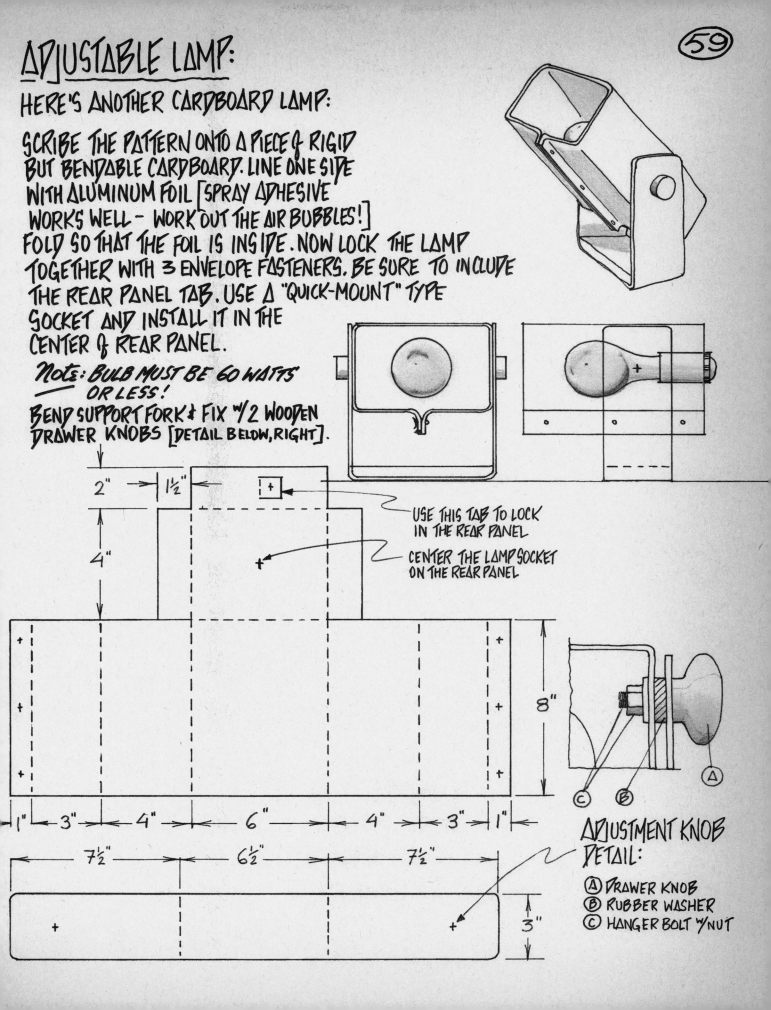

2"   1½"

4"

USE THIS TAB TO LOCK IN THE REAR PANEL

CENTER THE LAMP SOCKET ON THE REAR PANEL

8"

1"   3"   4"   6"   4"   3"   1"

7½"   6½"   7½"

3"

ADJUSTMENT KNOB DETAIL:

Ⓐ DRAWER KNOB
Ⓑ RUBBER WASHER
Ⓒ HANGER BOLT w/ NUT

FRYING-PAN LAMP:

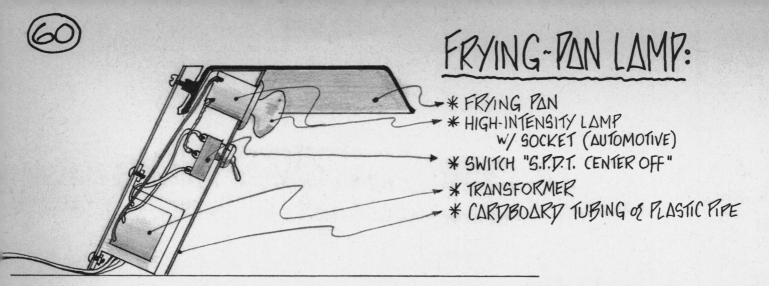

* FRYING PAN
* HIGH-INTENSITY LAMP W/ SOCKET (AUTOMOTIVE)
* SWITCH "S.P.D.T. CENTER OFF"
* TRANSFORMER
* CARDBOARD TUBING or PLASTIC PIPE

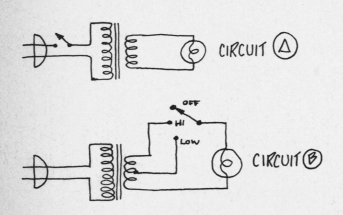

CIRCUIT Ⓐ

OFF
HI
LOW

CIRCUIT Ⓑ

A FRYING PAN IS A GOOD WAY of SHADING A "HIGH-HEAT-SOURCE," HIGH-INTENSITY-TYPE DESK LAMP. COMBINING AN INEXPENSIVE FRYING PAN WITH A FEW ELECTRONIC PARTS MAKES FOR A LAMP BOTH LOGICAL & UNIQUE.

➡ BUY EITHER A 6 VOLT or 12 VOLT BULB, BUT BE SURE TO BUY A TRANSFORMER THAT HAS THE SAME RATING AT ITS SECONDARY COIL. IF THE TRANSFORMER HAS A "CENTER TAP" YOU CAN USE CIRCUIT Ⓑ AND PROVIDE TWO LEVELS of ILLUMINATION. THE ABOVE ASSEMBLY DIAGRAM SHOWS THIS "HI-LOW" SITUATION.
CIRCUIT Ⓐ IS SIMPLY THE ADDITION of A LINE-CORD SWITCH.
AN [INSIDE SHINY] ALUMINUM PAN IS BEST. IF YOU DECIDE TO USE A CAST-IRON PAN or, WORSE YET, A TEFLON-LINED ONE, FIT THE INSIDE WITH AN ALUMINUM-FOIL CIRCLE.

DESK LAMP:

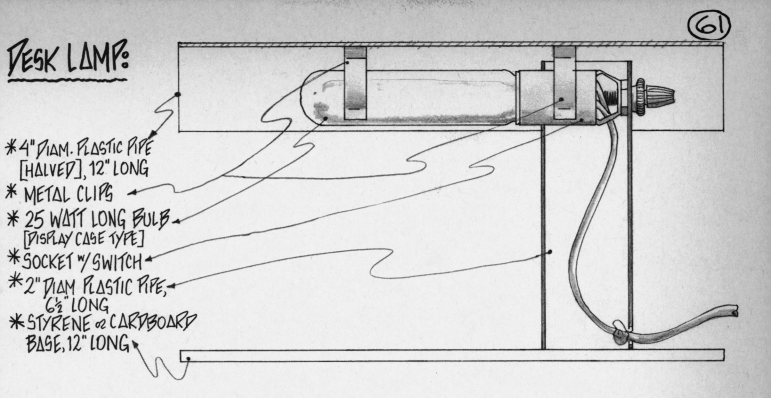

* 4" DIAM. PLASTIC PIPE [HALVED], 12" LONG
* METAL CLIPS
* 25 WATT LONG BULB [DISPLAY CASE TYPE]
* SOCKET w/ SWITCH
* 2" DIAM PLASTIC PIPE, 6½" LONG
* STYRENE or CARDBOARD BASE, 12" LONG

PROFILE & METAL CLIPS

Note: A HOLE IS MADE IN THE 2" DIAM. PLASTIC PIPE TO ACCEPT THE SOCKET. THE SOCKET IS AFFIXED BY DRILLING A MOUNTING HOLE IN THE REAR OF THE PIPE. THE SWITCH SECTION IS NOW INSERTED & LOCKED WITH THE KNURLED LOCK-NUT.

Note: LINE THE HALVED 4" DIAM. PLASTIC PIPE WITH ALUMINUM FOIL ON THE INSIDE. EITHER COVER THE OUTSIDE w/ MYLAR or PAINT IT TO YOUR TASTE.

THE WIRING IS STRAIGHT-FORWARD SINCE THE CORD ATTACHES DIRECTLY TO THE SOCKET.

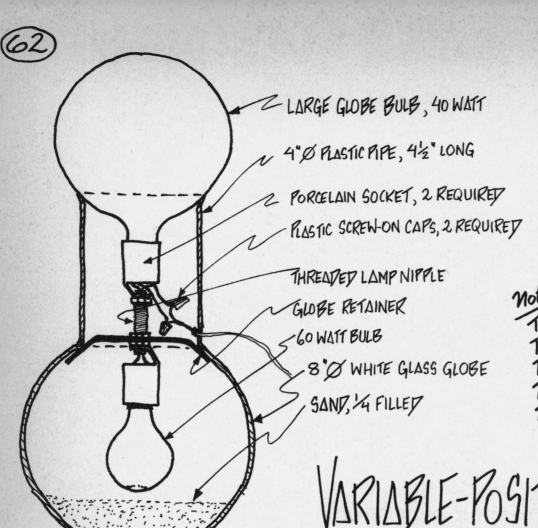

LARGE GLOBE BULB, 40 WATT

4"Ø PLASTIC PIPE, 4½" LONG

PORCELAIN SOCKET, 2 REQUIRED

PLASTIC SCREW-ON CAPS, 2 REQUIRED

THREADED LAMP NIPPLE

GLOBE RETAINER

60 WATT BULB

8"Ø WHITE GLASS GLOBE

SAND, ¼ FILLED

Note:
THE SYSTEM IS "LOCKED" TOGETHER BY SCREWING IN THE LARGE GLOBE BULB. THIS PUTS PRESSURE ON THE BOTTOM GLOBE RETAINER.

VARIABLE-POSITION DOUBLE-GLOBE LAMP:

THIS LAMP IS COMPLETELY EXPLAINED THROUGH ITS NAME & THE ASSEMBLY DRAWING. THE SAND WEIGHS IT DOWN ENOUGH TO MAKE DIFFERENT ANGLES POSSIBLE.

ADJUSTABLE DESK LAMP: 63

FOR A UNIQUE DESK LAMP, TAKE ADVAN-
TAGE OF MYLAR OR ALUMINUM FOIL.
THE LAMP CONSISTS OF A SMALL SPOT-
LIGHT MOUNTED IN A COFFEE CAN. THE
LIGHT SHINES A NARROW BEAM UPWARDS,
WHERE IT STRIKES THE REFLECTIVE
DISK. THE DISK [MYLAR OR ALUFOIL-
COVERED] IS HELD BY A MAGNET FOR
ADJUSTMENT. AN ACCURATE "ELLIPSE"
OF LIGHT CAN BE AIMED ANYWHERE
ON THE DESK SURFACE.
➡ GLUE A FERROUS CAP-NUT TO THE
BACKSIDE OF THE DISK FOR THE WIRE~
MOUNTED MAGNET. THE HALF-ROUND
OF THE CAP-NUT WILL ALLOW POSITIONS
AT ANY ANGLE. MOUNT THE SOCKET
AT THE BOTTOM OF THE CAN & USE A PAPER INSULATOR TO
PREVENT ELECTRIC SHORTS. USE A RUBBER GROMMET
WHERE THE CORD EXITS!

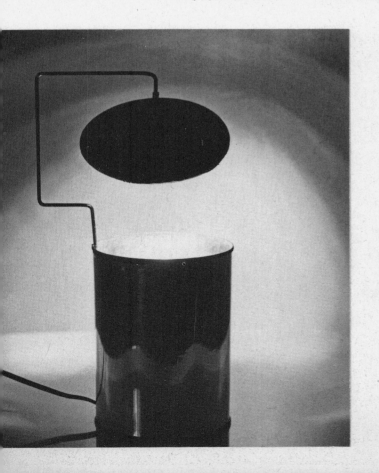

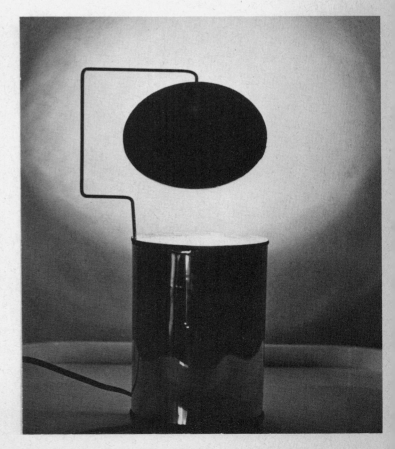

LAMP-SHADES

THERE IS NOTHING UNIQUE ABOUT THE IDEAS SHOWN ON THESE TWO PAGES. BUT THEY DEMONSTRATE HOW SIMPLY YOU CAN MAKE YOUR OWN DESIGN SOLUTIONS

GIVEN THE BASIC PLUG-CORD-SWITCH-SOCKET-BULB COMBINATION ➡ ALL YOU NEED TO COMPLETE THE LAMP IS SOME KIND OF A SHADE.

USUALLY SUSPENDED LAMPS ARE USED FOR GENERAL ISOLATED ILLUMINATION ➡ THE LIGHTING OF A TABLE OR THE CORNER OF A ROOM. SINCE SUCH A LAMP IS NOT "DIRECTABLE" IT IS NOT USUALLY USED FOR READING. AN OPEN-BOTTOM SHADE HAS BEEN FOUND GOOD FOR THIS PURPOSE.

↰ JIM MADE THIS LAMP OF AN OLD COLANDER. THE LEGS

AND HANDLES HAVE BEEN REMOVED AND THE OUTSIDE HAS BEEN SPRAYED FLAT BLACK.

THE INSIDE HAS BEEN KEPT AS IT WAS: THE ORIGINAL ALUMINUM SERVES WELL TO REFLECT MORE LIGHT.

WICKER & GRASS SIEVES, DEEP-FRY BASKETS or BASKETS FROM JAPAN & CHINA, COST VERY LITTLE. ONLY A MOUNTING HOLE WAS MADE IN THE CENTER BY JIM, THE BASKET REMAINS UNCHANGED. THE RESULTS ARE SURPRISINGLY GOOD.

NATURALLY THERE IS MUCH ELSE THAT COULD WORK AS A LAMPSHADE, FROM AN OLD FUNNEL TO YOUR OWN CARDBOARD CONSTRUCT. SO TRY YOUR OWN ➡ BUT BE CAREFUL ABOUT FLAMMABILITY!

STORAGE: [+ SYSTEMS]

OWNING THINGS MAKES BEING NOMADIC DIFFICULT.
BUT A LIFE WITHOUT POSSESSIONS IS NO LONGER REALIZABLE.
JIM & VIC, WHO CAN BY NOW CLAIM TO BE EXPERTS AT
MOVING THEIR FAMILIES & THEMSELVES, HAVE DIVIDED
THINGS THAT NEED STORAGE INTO SEVEN PILES:

1/ NECESSITIES THAT CAN & SHOULD BE PROTECTED FROM
DUST & VIEW [CLOTHING, TOOLS, CAMERAS, FILM]

2/ NECESSITIES TO BE "HIDDEN AWAY", BUT IN NEED OF
SEQUENTIAL FILING [FILES, DOCUMENTS, SLIDES, WORK]

3/ NECESSITIES THAT NEED TO BE LOCKED AWAY [DRUGS,
CLEANING FLUIDS, BLEACHES, OTHER CHEMICALS].

4/ NECESSITIES FOR WHICH STORAGE COMMONLY EXISTS IN
FLATS & ROOMS [FOODSTUFF, LINENS, COATS, ETC.]

5/ ROMANTIC NECESSITIES [CANDLES, PLANTS, INCENSE,
WINES, CALLIGRAPHIC SCREENS]

6/ SEMI-LUXURIES WE LIKE TO DISPLAY [BOOKS, RECORDS,
CERAMICS, GLASS, ETC.]

7/ SENTIMENTAL TRIVIA [WEDDING GIFTS, GREAT-GRANDPA'S
FLINTLOCK RIFLE, BABY SATU'S FIRST SHOES, ETC.]

WE HAVE TRIED TO MAKE SUGGESTIONS FOR THINGS
YOU MIGHT BUY, AS WELL AS PROVIDE YOU WITH DIAGRAMS
& INSTRUCTIONS of WHAT YOU CAN BUILD.

SINCE VIC HELPED WITH NOMADIC FURNITURE 1 ,
EXACTLY A YEAR AGO, HE HAS MOVED WITH HIS FAMILY
FROM SOUTHERN CALIFORNIA TO DENMARK; 11 MONTHS
LATER HE MOVED AGAIN: DENMARK TO ENGLAND.
BOTH MOVES WERE GOOD LEARNING EXPERIENCES, WELL
SUITED TO ELIMINATING THE SUPERFICIAL & TRIVIAL. BUT
MOVING WITH A 3½-YEAR-OLD, ONE ALSO SOON DISCOVERS
THE ABSOLUTE NEED FOR "ASSOCIATIONAL NECESSITIES": A
FAVOURITE TEDDY BEAR, A SECURITY BLANKET oz, IN THE
CASE of ADULTS, AN ESKIMO MASK oz A NAVAHO POT oz
SOME IMPORTANT BOOKS.

WE SERIOUSLY SUGGEST THAT, BEING A FELLOW~
NOMAD, YOU LOOK THROUGH ALL YOU HAVE AND GIVE AWAY,
SELL oz RECYCLE WHAT YOU CAN DO WITHOUT.

FINALLY, ONE TROUBLE WITH MOST STORAGE SYSTEMS
IS THAT THEY TOO MUST BE MOVED. THIS IS THE REASON
WE HAVE GIVEN SO MUCH SPACE TO RISTOMATTI RATIA'S
"PALASET": THE SYSTEM CAN BE MOVED FULL-PACKED.

AGAIN: FIND YOUR OWN SOLUTIONS & USE THIS
BOOK ONLY LIKE A DICTIONARY.

SIMPLEST SHELF SYSTEM:

THE HEART OF THIS SYSTEM IS A READILY
AVAILABLE FASTENER ——————⟶
AS YOU SEE,
THE FASTENERS LOOK LIKE A WOODSCREW
AT BOTH ENDS & COME IN VARIOUS LENGTHS.

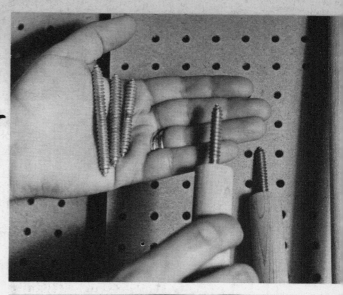

- THE UPRIGHTS ARE 1" Ø WOOD DOWELS,
  AVAILABLE IN 36" STANDARD LENGTH.
  CUT THESE HARDWOOD DOWELS INTO 12" &
  24" LENGTHS [*or any size that will
  work for your needs*].

- SHELVING COULD BE PLYWOOD, PRESS-
  BOARD, CHIPBOARD, MASONITE or
  HEAVY PEGBOARD ⅜" or THICKER.

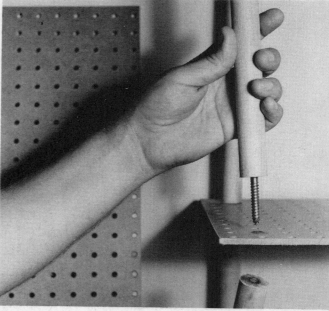

➤ DRILL PILOT HOLES INTO THE ENDS OF
  EACH DOWEL. THESE SHOULD BE
  HALF AS DEEP AS THE TOTAL LENGTH
  OF THE FASTENERS. [YOU CAN EASILY
  FIND THE CENTERS BY PLACING A 1"
  WASHER OVER THE END OF THE DOWEL
  & SCRIBING THE INSIDE CIRCLE WITH
  A PENCIL]. NEXT DRILL "THROUGH-
  HOLES" INTO THE CORNERS & PERHAPS
  CENTER EDGES OF SHELVING BOARDS.
  SOAP THE FASTENERS [THEY'LL GO
  IN MORE EASILY] & START ASSEMBLY.

*You will soon see that the
system allows for enormous
variation.*

Canvas Wall Pockets:

IN OUR EARLIER BOOK WE SUGGESTED WALL POCKETS & ROOM DIVIDERS WITH POCKETS, MADE OF CANVAS. BY NOW SUCH THINGS ARE PRODUCED COMMERCIALLY. NONETHELESS, HERE ARE SOME IDEA SKETCHES:

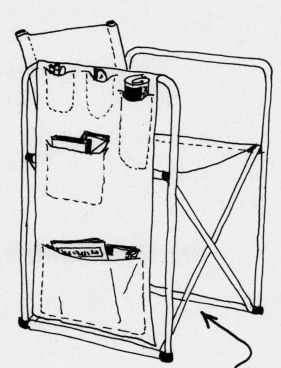

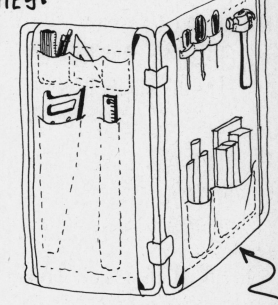

SHOP-TOOL STORAGE DIVIDER

CHAIR STORAGE

Note: USE HEAVY CANVAS, FASTEN TO WALL OR ROOM-DIVIDER POLES WITH BRASS GUSSETS.

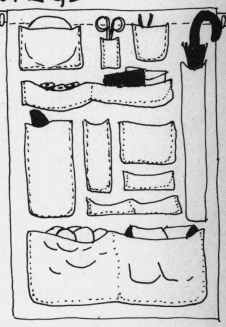

SCRAP-CLOTH STORAGE

PALASET

RISTOMATTI RATIA OF FINLAND DESIGNED THIS SYSTEM. IN VIC'S OPINION IT IS BY FAR THE MOST VERSATILE RANGE OF STORAGE UNITS EVER INVENTED. WHILE SOMEWHAT EXPENSIVE, THE SYSTEM HAS MANY UNUSUAL ADVANTAGES FOR NOMADIC LIVING:

* CUBES & DRAWERS ARE MADE OF TOUGH [YET LIGHTWEIGHT] PLASTIC [INJECTION-MOULDED STRUCTURAL POLYSTYRENE] & WILL HOLD UP WELL FOR DECADES - INCLUDING MOVING.

* THEY ARE PAINTED [IN 5 BRIGHT COLOURS] SO AS NOT TO ATTRACT DUST, AS MOST PLASTICS DO. MATERIAL CONTROL IS RIGID → PLASTIC DOESN'T WARP IN DAMP CLIMATES.

* THE UNITS CAN EASILY BE PAINTED, DRILLED, SAWN WITH HAND TOOLS.

* EACH CUBE COMES IN A STURDY CARDBOARD BOX WITH PLASTIC CORNER BRACES. VIC HAS RETAINED THE BOXES → WHEN MOVING DAY COMES, THE CUBES, INCLUDING DRAWERS & CONTENTS, CAN MOVE [DRAWER HANDLES DETACH]: ENTIRE FILING & TOOL SYSTEMS CAN THUS BE MOVED IN ORDER.

YOU CAN START WITH ONE CUBE, WHICH MIGHT MAKE A TELEPHONE TABLE OR PLANTER BOX & THEN ADD TO YOUR SYSTEM.

* CUBES ARE STRONG ENOUGH TO SUPPORT A MAN [WITH A SQUARE FOAM CUSHION THEY MAKE GOOD SEATS] OR TO BE SCRIBED TO A WALL AS HANGING STORAGE SHELVING.

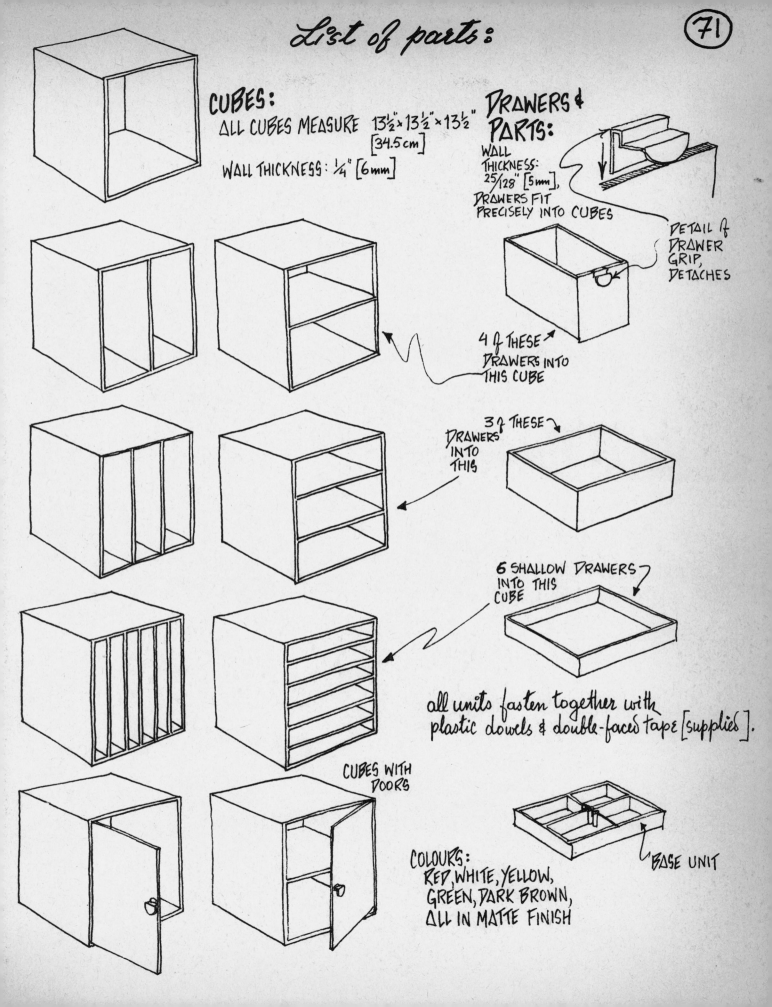

CUBES:
ALL CUBES MEASURE 13½" × 13½" × 13½" [34.5cm]

WALL THICKNESS: ¼" [6mm]

DRAWERS & PARTS:
WALL THICKNESS: 25/128" [5mm], DRAWERS FIT PRECISELY INTO CUBES

DETAIL OF DRAWER GRIP, DETACHES

4 OF THESE DRAWERS INTO THIS CUBE

3 OF THESE DRAWERS INTO THIS

6 SHALLOW DRAWERS INTO THIS CUBE

all units fasten together with plastic dowels & double-faced tape [supplies].

CUBES WITH DOORS

BASE UNIT

COLOURS:
RED, WHITE, YELLOW, GREEN, DARK BROWN, ALL IN MATTE FINISH

THE CUBES & DRAWERS COME IN A FLAT, MATTE FINISH. CUBES IN WHITE OR A VERY DARK BROWN [*nearly* BLACK]. THE DRAWERS ALSO COME IN WHITE & BROWN, AS WELL AS A ZIPPY RED, A CHROME-STRONG YELLOW & A RATHER REGRETTABLE GREEN. THIS MAKES COLOUR-CODING OF FILES & OTHER MATERIALS POSSIBLE. OF COURSE THERE ARE MANY OTHER OPTIONS: CUBES CAN WORK EITHER VERTICALLY OR HORIZONTALLY. THE 13½" SIZE WILL ACCEPT L.P. RECORDS & ALBUMS. OPEN CUBES CAN CONVERT TO SPEAKER ENCLOSURES [BELOW].

SOME OF THE DRAWERS CAN ALSO BE MOUNTED UPRIGHT ON WALLS TO PROVIDE A SERIES OF SHALLOW SHELVES OR SHADOW BOXES. AS THE SURFACES ARE EMINENTLY PAINTABLE, YOUR IMAGINATION IS THE ONLY LIMIT.

VIC USES THE SHALLOW 6-DRAWER UNITS AS HORIZONTAL FILING
FOR MANUSCRIPTS-IN-PROGRESS, PHOTOGRAPHIC WORK, CORRESPONDENCE
& PAPERS, DESIGN WORK, PAPERS, PENCILS & TOOLS. THE BIG ADVANTAGE
OF THE SYSTEM LIES IN BEING ABLE TO JUST SHOVE ALL OF THE ABOVE
INTO 22 REINFORCED CARDBOARD BOXES & SHIP AS IS. THIS WAS
DONE FROM CALIFORNIA TO DENMARK AND, MORE RECENTLY, FROM
KØBENHAVN TO CHESHIRE IN ENGLAND. ASSEMBLY TIME FOR THE
UNUSUALLY LARGE UNIT ABOVE IS ABOUT
2 HOURS, FOR ONE PERSON. SIZES OF L.P.^{S},
PORTABLE TYPEWRITERS, FILM CANS, 10" TAPE
REELS, STANDARD PAPER SIZES, ETC., WERE ALL CONSIDERED IN
DEVELOPING THE SIZES OF CUBES & COMPONENTS.

PLASTIC DOWEL, TWICE
ACTUAL SIZE, WHICH
HOLDS CUBES TOGETHER.

AS YOU CAN SEE BELOW, EVEN STANDARD WINE & WHISKEY BOTTLE HEIGHTS, GLASSES & EXTRA-LENGTH PROFESSIONAL STUDIO TAPE REELS FIT SNUGLY. AVAILABLE FROM SHOPS IN MANY COUNTRIES, SPECIFICALLY: THE HABITAT CHAIN, IN BRITAIN
FORM & FARVE, DENMARK
DESIGN RESEARCH, U.S.A.

Palaset won the "Furniture of the Year" award for 1972/73 in the Nordic countries - a tough audience indeed.

MADE BY:

TRESTON O.Y.
SORATIE 1
20720 TURKU 72
FINLAND

TRESTON LTD.
UNIT 2A
HYTHE ROAD INDUSTRIAL ESTATE
LONDON NW 10, ENGLAND

SOME FINAL THOUGHTS ON CUBES & PALASET:

AS NOTED EARLIER, PALASET IS EXPENSIVE. HOWEVER, IT IS EXPENSIVE ONLY IF YOU GO OUT & BUY, SAY, 60 CUBES AND 45 CUBE~GUTS TO FURNISH A TRENDY HOME. IF YOU TRY TO THINK OF IT AS A <u>PERMANENT</u> <u>FILING-STORAGE-SHIPPING-CRATE SYSTEM</u> THE PRICE BECOMES UNDER~STANDABLE. SINCE THIS BOOK IS ABOUT NOMADICS, WE AGAIN STRESS THE SHEER DELIGHT OF MOVING FROM ONE COUNTRY TO ANOTHER & ON ARRIVAL HAVING ALL FILES, CORRESPONDENCE, RECORDS, PHOTOS, TAPES, ETC. [INCLUDING THE WORK FOR THIS BOOK] STILL IN CORRECT SEQUENCE.

IF YOU WISH TO BUILD YOUR OWN CUBE SYSTEM, HOWEVER, YOU MIGHT WORK IN PRESSBOARD [SEE KEN YOST'S CUBES, PAGE 128] OR IN TRIPLE-PLY CORRUGATED CARDBOARD. AN <u>INTERIOR</u> CUBE MEASUREMENT WILL BE IDEAL AT <u>13¼"</u> THIS WILL TAKE MOST LARGER ITEMS: L.P. RECORDS IN COLLECTOR'S ALBUMS W/ SLIPCASES, WINE BOTTLES, PROFESSIONAL TAPE REELS. IT WILL IN THIS SIZE ALSO SUB-DIVIDE DOWN EASILY TO ACCEPT CASSETTE TAPES, 35mm & 2½ × 2½ SLIDE SERIES, VIDEO TAPE, ALL BUT THE LARGEST ART BOOKS, STANDARD-SIZED STATIONERY [A4 IN EUROPE]. BRASS RIVET PINS USED FOR MAILING ENVELOPES CAN SECURE CUBE TO CUBE & ALSO "BUTTON THROUGH" TO SECURE BOTH VERTICAL DIVIDERS & SHELVES WITHIN THE CUBES. PAINT OR COVER WITH CONTACT PAPER or FABRIC.

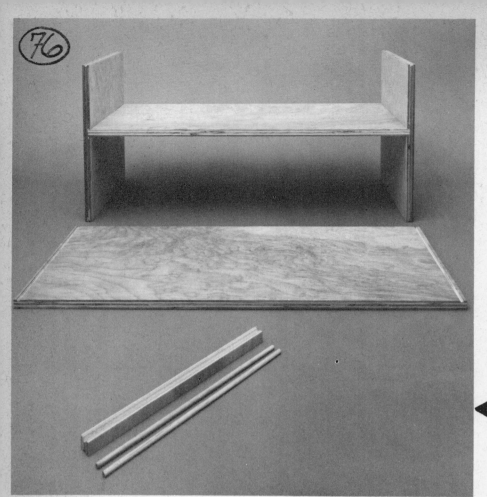

"H" MODULE SYSTEM:

CHARLES ANACKER [ONE OF JIM'S STUDENTS] DEVELOPED THIS BOOKSHELF SYSTEM.
IT IS COMPOSED OF "H"-SHAPED MODULES, WOODEN DOWELS, EXTRA SHELVES, AND FILLER PIECES.

AN AMAZING VARIETY OF COMBINATIONS CAN BE CONSTRUCTED AND, BECAUSE OF THE SIMPLICITY OF THIS SYSTEM, VERY INEXPENSIVELY. IN THIS PHOTO YOU CAN SEE HOW THE DOWEL RODS FIT INTO ROUTED SLOTS TO "LOCK" EACH MODULE.

EXTRA SHELF UNITS CAN BE ADDED TO THE "H" MODULES TO EXTEND THE SYSTEM SIDEWAYS. FILLER PIECES [ALSO SEEN] MAINTAIN SPACING WHEN AN EXTRA SHELF IS ADDED.

THIS CUTTING DIAGRAM SHOWS THAT
CONSTRUCTION COULDN'T BE EASIER.
FOR SIMPLICITY, WE'VE ROUNDED OFF
THE DIMENSIONS TO WHOLE NUMBERS.
WHEN CUTTING THE PANEL, HOWEVER,
BE SURE TO INCLUDE THE WIDTH of
THE SAW-BLADE.

96"

32"

16"

12" · 12" · 12" · 12"

48"

DETAILING of INTERLOCK BETWEEN 2 "H" MODULES
[ENDS ONLY] AND DOWEL "LOCK":

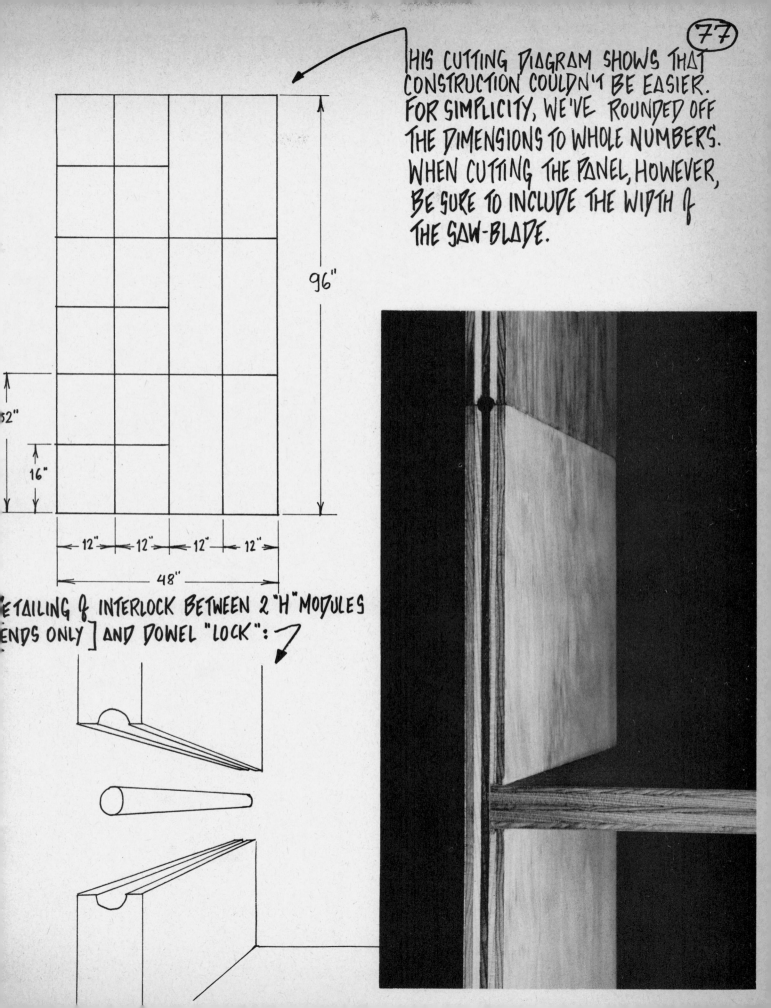

FOR EXTRA STRENGTH, THE MODULES ARE DADOED [SLOTTED] TO FIT THE CROSSPIECE.

YOU CAN GET SIX FULL MODULES FROM EACH 4×8 FOOT SHEET OF PLYWOOD.

AT THAT PRICE YOU CAN EASILY FILL ANY WALL OF YOUR PLACE WITH THESE SHELVING UNITS.

AS THIS LAST PHOTO SHOWS, YOU CAN ALSO EXPAND THE SYSTEM IN A UNIQUE WAY: IT SHOWS HOW THE ADDITION OF EXTRA SHELVES CAN PROVIDE "IN-BETWEEN" STORAGE WHEN USED WITH TWO TOWERS OF FOUR UNITS EACH.

➡ USE VENEERED PLYWOOD IF YOU WANT AN EXCEPTIONALLY FINE-LOOKING SYSTEM.

WITH THE BEST of INTENTIONS TO REMAIN FREE of POSSESSIONS, WE EVENTUALLY STILL AMASS BEAUTIFUL TRIVIA: SEA SHELLS, OLD COINS, A SINGLE NAVAJO EARRING, A NICE STONE ... AND WE VALUE THESE FEW THINGS FOR THEIR AESTHETIC or ROMANTIC or ASSOCIATIONAL APPEAL.
TROUBLE IS THEY ARE USUALLY STUCK AMONG THE LEVIS OR THE FORKS.

TYPESETTERS USE THESE HANDSOME DRAWERS ↑ TO KEEP THEIR TYPE NEAT. A NEWSPAPER OUT IN THE STICKS OFTEN JUST PITCHES THEM. THEY'RE MADE of WOOD & DESERVE TO BE RECYCLED.

"⑧⓪ the closet":

IN MOST AMERICAN AND EUROPEAN OLDER APARTMENTS, CLOSET SPACE DOESN'T EXIST AT ALL.

CARDBOARD CLOSETS or THOSE PLASTIC CLOTH ZIP-TOGETHER HORRORS, AVAILABLE AT DEPARTMENT STORES, HAVE A TENDENCY TO BECOME UNSTUCK, JAM or FALL APART AFTER MORE THAN A YEAR of HARD USE.

HERE ARE SOME IDEAS FOR "CLOSET" PARTS THAT WILL MOVE & ADJUST TO MOST CEILING HEIGHTS.

➡ THE UPRIGHT PANELS COULD BE HOLLOW~ CORE DOORS ["ONE-SIDE-DAMAGED" ARE CHEAP FROM BUILDING CONTRACTORS] or ELSE $^{15}/_{16}$" THICK PLYWOOD or CHIPBOARD PANELS, 84"×24". ➡

USE FOUR 12" CARRIAGE BOLTS PER PANEL AS LEGS & TOPS, AS SHOWN, BY DRILLING <u>DOWN</u> INTO PANEL TOP-EDGE & <u>UP</u> INTO <u>BOTTOM-EDGE</u> ABOUT 5". MAKE 4 ROUND ACCESS HOLES, ABOUT 1" Ø, IN EACH PANEL & POP A HEXAGONAL NUT IN <u>BEFORE</u> SLIDING THE BOLT IN.

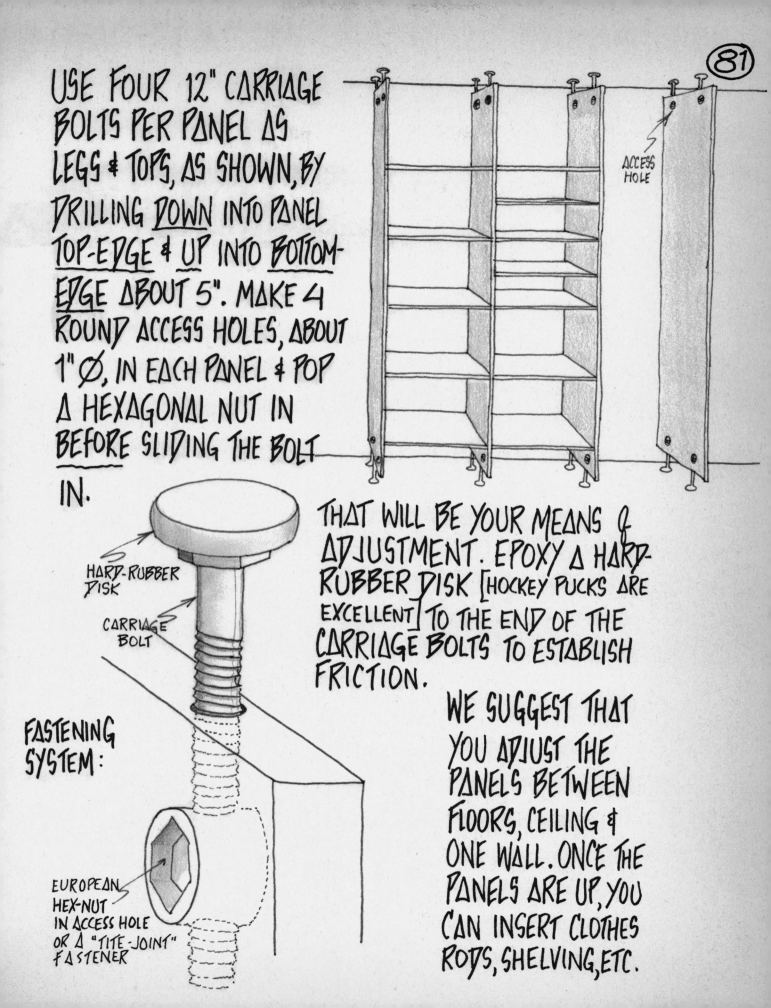

ACCESS HOLE

HARD-RUBBER DISK

CARRIAGE BOLT

FASTENING SYSTEM:

EUROPEAN HEX-NUT IN ACCESS HOLE OR A "TITE-JOINT" FASTENER

THAT WILL BE YOUR MEANS OF ADJUSTMENT. EPOXY A HARD-RUBBER DISK [HOCKEY PUCKS ARE EXCELLENT] TO THE END OF THE CARRIAGE BOLTS TO ESTABLISH FRICTION.

WE SUGGEST THAT YOU ADJUST THE PANELS BETWEEN FLOORS, CEILING & ONE WALL. ONCE THE PANELS ARE UP, YOU CAN INSERT CLOTHES RODS, SHELVING, ETC.

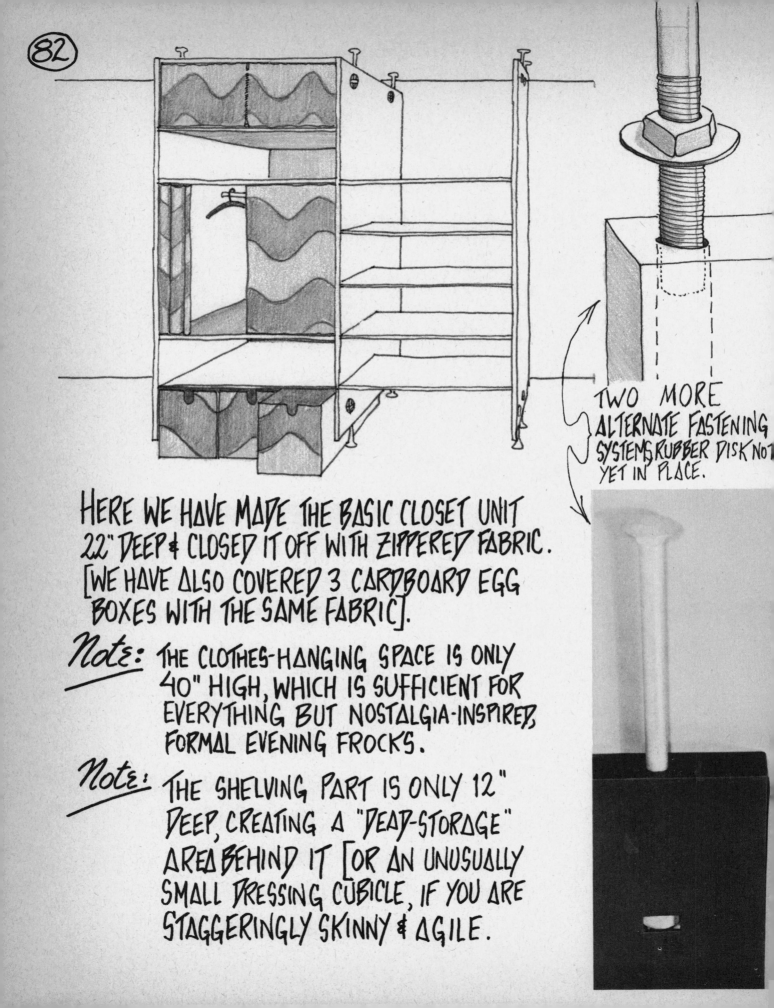

TWO MORE ALTERNATE FASTENING SYSTEMS. RUBBER DISK NOT YET IN PLACE.

HERE WE HAVE MADE THE BASIC CLOSET UNIT 22" DEEP & CLOSED IT OFF WITH ZIPPERED FABRIC. [WE HAVE ALSO COVERED 3 CARDBOARD EGG BOXES WITH THE SAME FABRIC].

Note: THE CLOTHES-HANGING SPACE IS ONLY 40" HIGH, WHICH IS SUFFICIENT FOR EVERYTHING BUT NOSTALGIA-INSPIRED, FORMAL EVENING FROCKS.

Note: THE SHELVING PART IS ONLY 12" DEEP, CREATING A "DEAD-STORAGE" AREA BEHIND IT [OR AN UNUSUALLY SMALL DRESSING CUBICLE, IF YOU ARE STAGGERINGLY SKINNY & AGILE.

WE KEEP PUSHING PAPER, RECYCLED PAPER & CARDBOARD.
REASON IS: PLASTICS ARE EXPENSIVE & NOT FULLY BIO-
DEGRADABLE AS YET, WOOD IS GROWING SCARCE.
THESE STANDARD DOCUMENT & OFFICE FILE BOXES
SELL AS FLAT SHEETS & USER~ASSEMBLED. THE SYSTEM
IS CALLED "ARCHIBOX" [A HOKEY LABEL FOR A GOOD
PRODUCT]. THE BOX SIZE IS $9\frac{1}{4}" \times 12\frac{3}{4}" \times 2\frac{1}{4}"$, MAKING
THE SYSTEM USEFUL FOR CLOTHES & CLUTTER AT HOME
TOO. VERY STURDY & LESS THAN 20¢ EACH!

 COLON EMBALLAGE
TAGENSVEJ 135
COPENHAGEN, DENMARK

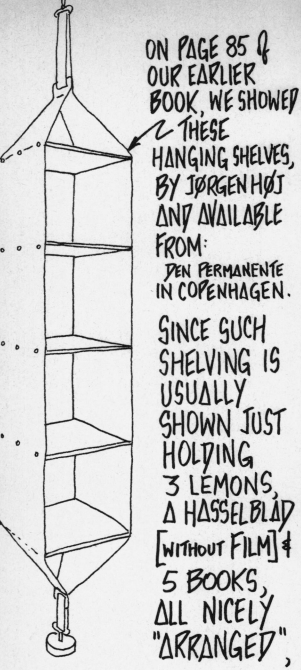

ON PAGE 85 of
OUR EARLIER
BOOK, WE SHOWED
THESE
HANGING SHELVES,
BY JØRGEN HØJ
AND AVAILABLE
FROM:
DEN PERMANENTE
IN COPENHAGEN.

SINCE SUCH
SHELVING IS
USUALLY
SHOWN JUST
HOLDING
3 LEMONS,
A HASSELBLAD
[WITHOUT FILM] &
5 BOOKS,
ALL NICELY
"ARRANGED",

VIC DID A LOAD TEST. HERE IS THE OUTCOME: THE
UNIT HAS HELD 235 POUNDS f RECORDS FOR A YEAR
AND, IN THE COURSE f ANY GIVEN EVENING, RECORDS
WOULD CONTINUALLY BE PULLED IN & OUT. [235 POUNDS
IS ABOUT THE WEIGHT f HANGING CLOTHING FOR TWO
PEOPLE ~ SO HOW ABOUT DEVELOPING A ZIPPERED CLOSET?]

SNAP-TOGETHER STORAGE CUBES:

YOU WILL NEED NO GLUE or FASTENERS! MAKE IT OUT of ¼" or ⅜" PLYWOOD. FIRST ASSEMBLE THE TWO SIDES Ⓐ AND THE BOTTOM, THEN SLIDE EACH SIDE Ⓑ INTO PLACE BY BENDING THEM OUT, OVER THE TABS, UNTIL TABS SNAP INTO PLACE.

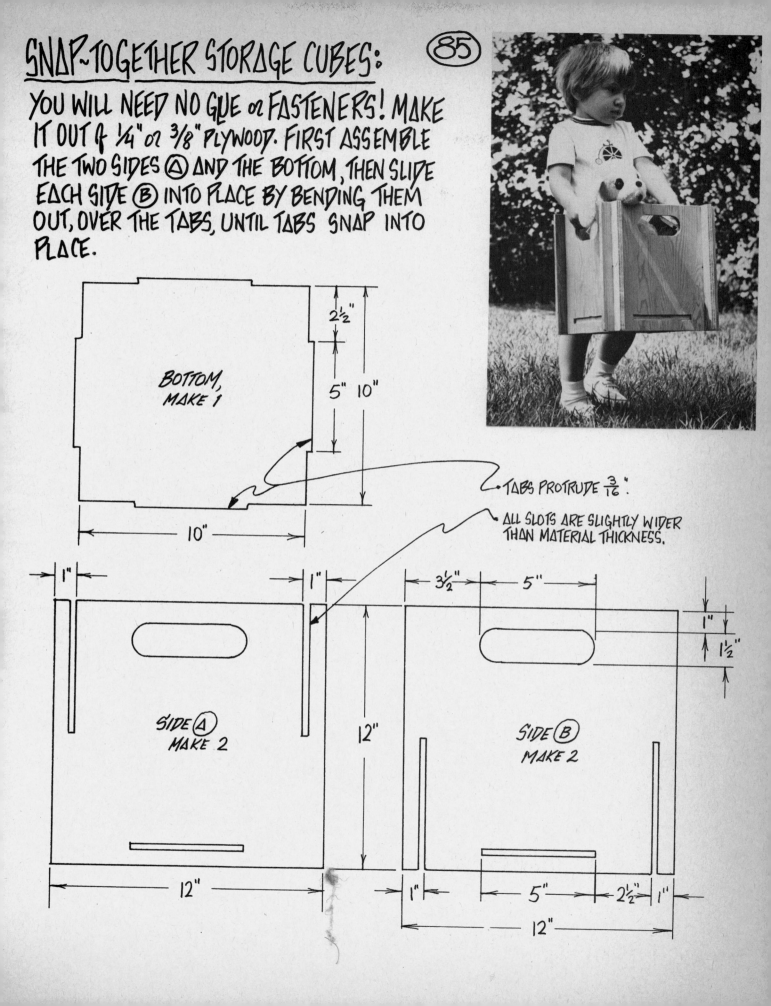

BOTTOM, MAKE 1

2½"

5" 10"

10"

TABS PROTRUDE 3/16".

ALL SLOTS ARE SLIGHTLY WIDER THAN MATERIAL THICKNESS.

1"   1"   3½"   5"   1"   1½"

SIDE Ⓐ MAKE 2   12"   SIDE Ⓑ MAKE 2

12"   1"   5"   2½"   1"

12"

CHILDREN:

WE'VE DECIDED TO BEGIN THIS CHAPTER WITH THIS TIRE SWING: A GREAT EXAMPLE of INNOVATION, RECYCLING & DESIGN SENSIBILITY.

THIS SWING IS JUST ONE of MANY FINE RECYCLED PRODUCTS DESIGNED BY GARY COLLINS & RANDY PRIDGEN, WHO ARE:

THE NATURALIST
P.O. BOX 1423
PROVO, UTAH 84601, U.S.A.

IF YOU'RE IN THE BIG APPLE, YOU CAN BUY THE SWING FROM THEM oz BLOOMINGDALE'S, IN THE HOUSEWARES DEPARTMENT.

BABiES + SMALL KiDS:

PARENTS ARE A REAL SUCKER~MARKET [GRANDPARENTS ARE WORSE], EASY PREY TO MANUFACTURERS & THEIR SNAKE~OIL BRIGADE FROM MADISON AVENUE. PRODUCTS TEND TO BE SLEAZY OR DANGEROUS [LIKE FLAMMABLE NIGHT~CLOTHING]. LIKE ADULTS, BABIES & SMALL CHILDREN CAN MAKE DO WITH A GREAT DEAL LESS. [AND SHOULD: AN AVERAGE AMERICAN BABY

CONSUMES 54 TIMES AS MANY PRODUCTS AS, SAY, A CHILD IN CHINA]. WE FEEL THAT MUCH CAN BE HOME-BUILT OR HOME-SEWN.

SO WE HAVE LISTED ONLY A FEW MANUFACTURED PRODUCTS. AMONG THESE IS THE STROLLER ABOVE, WHICH FOLDS DOWN TO NEARLY UMBRELLA~SIZE. IT COMES IN TWO SIZES; TYPES ARE MADE IN JAPAN, HONG KONG, BRITAIN, FRANCE & THE U.S. IT IS UNIVERSALLY AVAILABLE & IDEAL for FLYING, TRAVELLING & MOVING.

A "DAISY-CHAIN" TIRES HANGS FROM BURLAP-COVERED TELEPHONE POLES.

SMALLER POLES SUPPORT TIRES W/ LONG BOLTS & SHEAR PLATES ON THE INSIDE.

TIRE PLAYGROUND:

JIM LOCATED THIS PLAYGROUND AT ROSEDELL ELEMENTARY SCHOOL IN SAUGUS, CALIFORNIA. THE SCHOOL'S PRINCIPAL, DR. WHEELER, SAID THEIR VARIATION WAS ADAPTED FROM A PLAYGROUND AT THE LINDA VISTA SCHOOL IN PASADENA, CALIFORNIA. WE WERE UNABLE TO FIND OUT WHO FIRST DESIGNED IT. ➡ IT WAS A REAL COMMUNITY-INVOLVEMENT PROJECT: 15 PARENTS & TEACHERS WORKED FOR ABOUT 1½ MONTHS & WERE LATER HELPED BY HIRED SCHOOL STUDENTS. ABOUT 5 PARENTS & TEACHERS WORKED ON THE WHOLE PROJECT FROM CONCEPTION ON.

LARGE TIRES. KIDS CAN CLIMB UP OR THROUGH. SECOND LAYER OF TIRES TO BE FILLED WITH SAND SO CHILDREN CAN JUMP DOWN W/O INJURY.

CARGO-NET OF ATTACHED TIRES LEADS TO AN ELEVATED PLATFORM FROM WHICH KIDS CAN EXIT VIA TWO FIRE-POLES. 89

THE OLD TIRES WERE LOCAL. GOODYEAR CONTRIBUTED THE EXTRA-LARGE TIRES AT NO COST BUT ABOUT $120.- HAD TO BE PAID TO TRUCK THEM IN. THE TOTAL PLAYGROUND COST ABOUT $800.-

CONTRAST THAT WITH THE FACT THAT JUST ONE CONVENTIONAL SWING-SET [4 SWINGS & 1 SLIDE] COSTS NEARLY $1000.- UNINSTALLED!

WE'VE INCLUDED THIS CASE HISTORY TO TURN YOU ON TO COMMUNITY ACTION USING RECYCLED OR "JUNK" MATERIALS. IF THE COMMUNITY YOU'VE JUST MOVED TO LACKS A PLAYGROUND [OR WHATEVER] DON'T KEEP ON COMPLAINING ◆ BUILD ONE WITH YOUR NEIGHBOURS & SHARE THE RESULTS WITH OTHER COMMUNITIES!

THE ALMOST ARCHETYPAL BACK-YARD TIRE SWING.

THE KAYAK~SACK:*

*KAJAKPOSEN

UNFORTUNATELY MANY CHILDREN STRANGLE EACH YEAR IN HARNESSES & OTHER DEVICES IN PRAMS, COTS OR PERAMBULATORS.

STARTING WITH THE CONCEPT f AN ESKIMO, WARM & DRY IN HIS KAYAK, AASE RAAGAARD HAS DEVELOPED THIS SACK WHICH CAN FIT INTO PERAMBULATORS & IS ALSO AVAILABLE WITH ADAPTORS FOR COTS & BEDS. IT KEEPS BABIES WARM & DRY & ALSO PREVENTS ACCIDENTAL STRANGULATION. IT HAS BEEN TESTED BY MEDICAL & CHILD-CARE PEOPLE SINCE 1966 & BEEN FOUND SUPERIOR & SAFER TO ANYTHING SIMILAR on THE MARKET. Don't make your own!

IN MARCH f 1973, AASE RAAGAARD SAW VIC ON DANISH T.V. AND WROTE: "Dr. BENGT-ZACHAU-CHRISTIANSEN, NURSERY SUPERVISOR ODA ANDERSEN & I - CONSIDERED SENDING OUT PATTERNS f THE KAYAK-SACK - BUT WE DARE NOT!

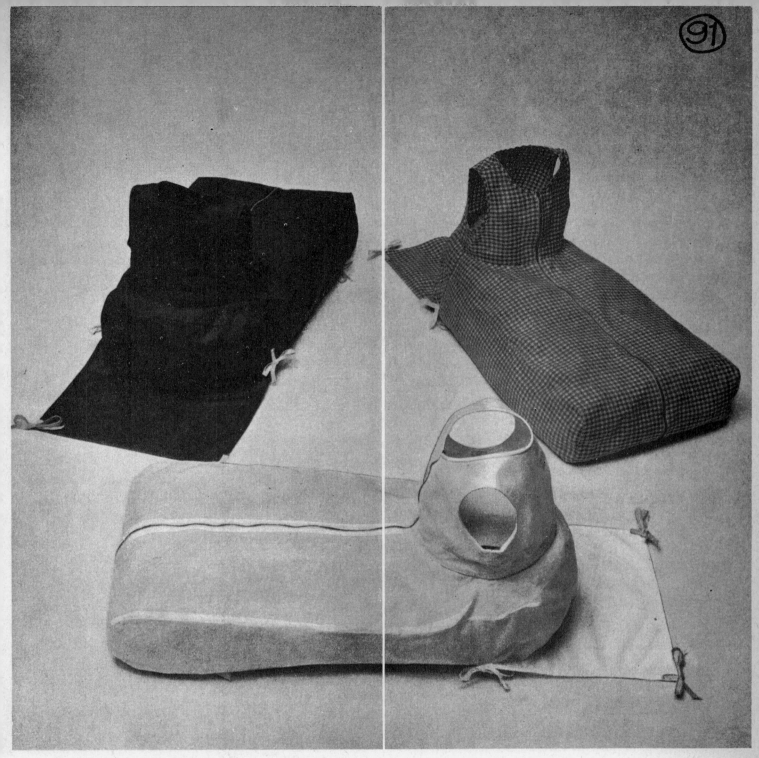

IT IS DIFFICULT TO SEW, MUST BE DONE CONSCIENTIOUSLY, AND A CONSUMER-PROTECTION MAGAZINE WARNS: "DON'T USE HOME-MADE STRINGS." THE SAME MAGAZINE ALSO HAS CALLED THE KAYAK-SACK "THE *ONLY* IDIOT-SAFE CHILDREN'S THING".

BUY FROM ➡ AASE RAAGAARD
5900 RUDKØBING
DENMARK

ROCKER FOR TWO CHILDREN:

FIRST DRAW THE TWO SMALL CIRCLES [16" DIAMETER EACH] ON THE 48"×24" BOARD. CONNECT THE CENTERS OF BOTH CIRCLES AND DIVIDE THIS LINE IN HALF: THIS IS THE CENTER OF THE LARGE CIRCLE [ABOUT 24" DIAMETER].

THE 3 TRIANGLES ARE GLUED IN TO KEEP THE CORRECT ANGLE OF THE TWO MAIN PIECES & THE TWO

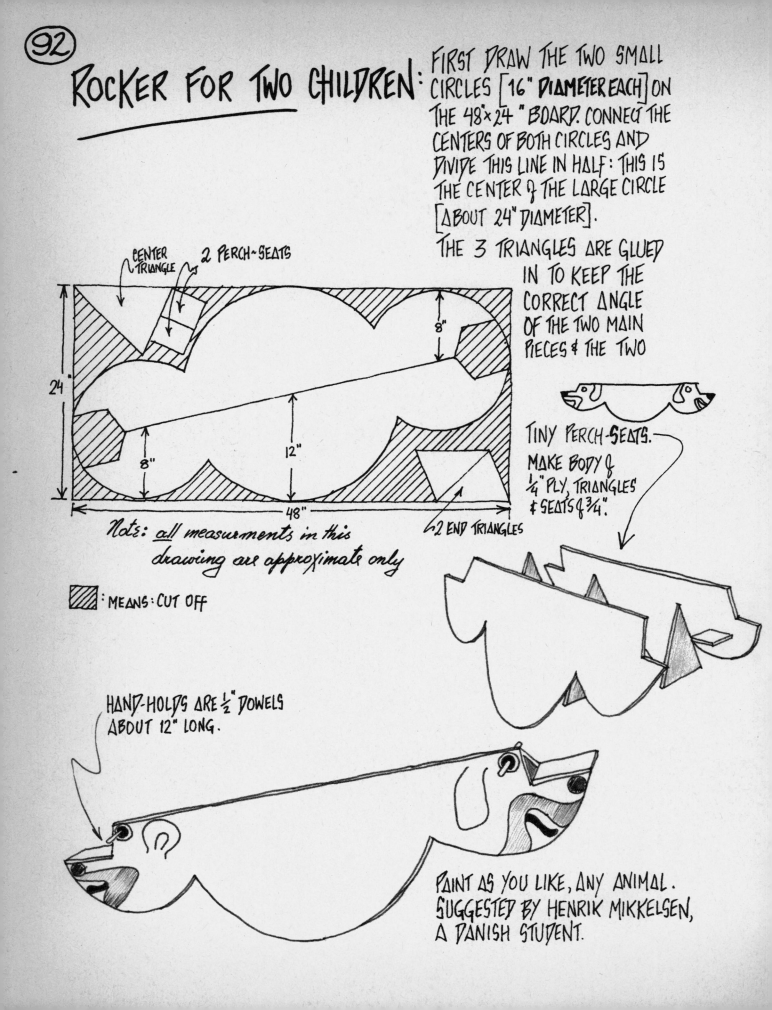

CENTER TRIANGLE

2 PERCH~SEATS

24"

8"

8"

12"

48"

Note: <u>all</u> measurements in this drawing are approximate only

⬛ : MEANS: CUT OFF

2 END TRIANGLES

TINY PERCH-SEATS. MAKE BODY OF ¼" PLY, TRIANGLES & SEATS OF ¾".

HAND-HOLDS ARE ½" DOWELS ABOUT 12" LONG.

PAINT AS YOU LIKE, ANY ANIMAL. SUGGESTED BY HENRIK MIKKELSEN, A DANISH STUDENT.

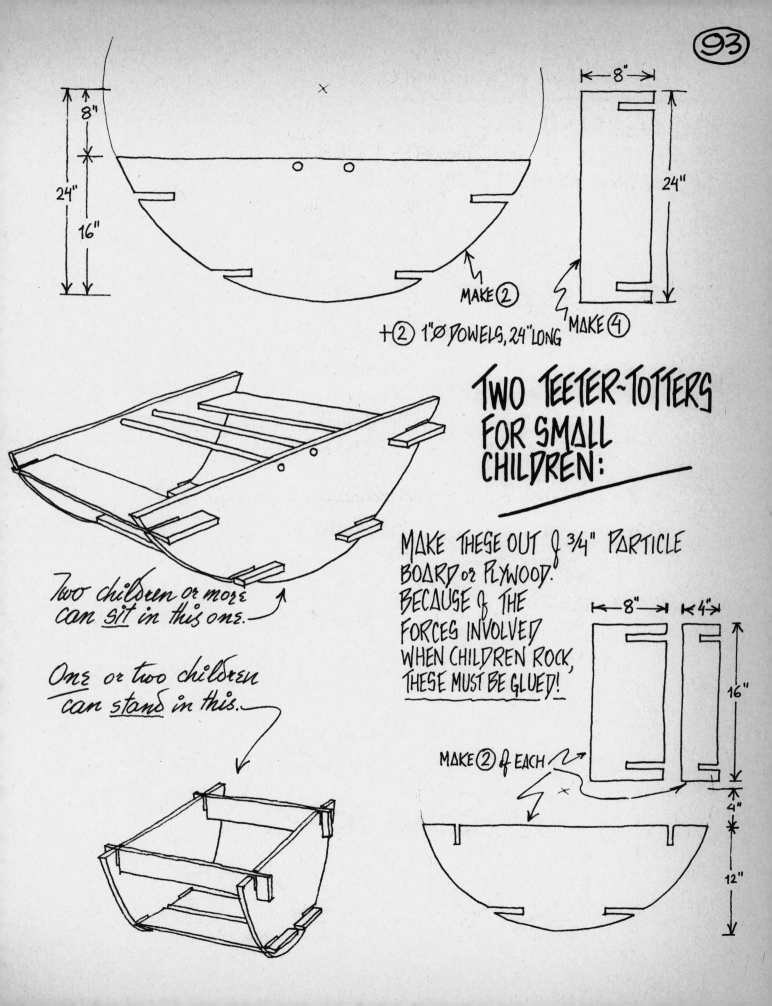

8"

24"

16"

×

8"

24"

MAKE ②

+ ② 1"∅ DOWELS, 24" LONG

MAKE ④

TWO TEETER-TOTTERS FOR SMALL CHILDREN:

Two children or more can sit in this one.

One or two children can stand in this.

MAKE THESE OUT ƒ ¾" PARTICLE BOARD or PLYWOOD. BECAUSE ƒ THE FORCES INVOLVED WHEN CHILDREN ROCK, THESE MUST BE GLUED!

8" ⊢ 4" ⊣

16"

MAKE ② ƒ EACH

4"

12"

3-WAY SHAPES for CHILDREN:

MAKE THESE PLAY~WORK SHAPES OF ½" PLYWOOD. THEN ASSEMBLE THE TWO CROSSPIECES & SCREW THE ENDS ON. YOU MIGHT DECIDE TO GLUE & NAIL THEM ON INSTEAD, TO MAKE THE UNITS MORE PERMANENT.

➤ THE TWO SEAT HEIGHTS ACCOMMODATE GROWING CHILDREN. THESE SHAPES ARE ALSO GREAT FOR STORAGE, CLIMBING & IMAGINATIVE FUN.

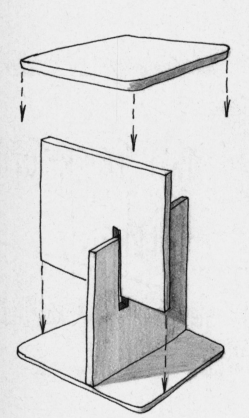

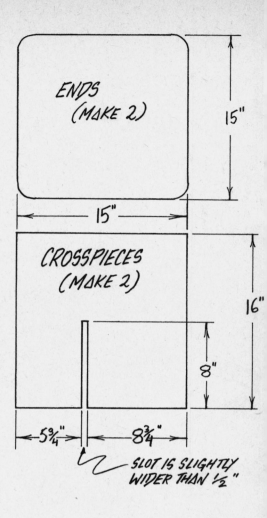

ENDS (MAKE 2)

15"

15"

CROSSPIECES (MAKE 2)

16"

8"

5¾"   8¾"

SLOT IS SLIGHTLY WIDER THAN ½"

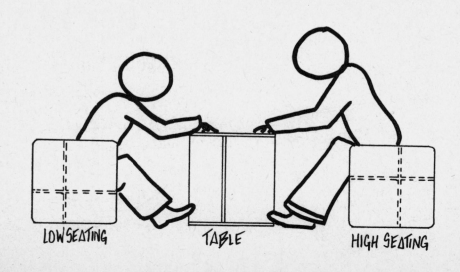

LOW SEATING   TABLE   HIGH SEATING

PLAY or WORK TABOURET:

THESE TABOURETS CAN BE USED NEXT TO A DRAFTING TABLE, FOR TOOLS, OR AS KIDS' PLAY UNITS. MADE of CARDBOARD or FIBRE-BOARD CYLINDERS, TRAYS SWING OUT. IF YOU WISH, YOU CAN ADD RECESSED CASTERS,

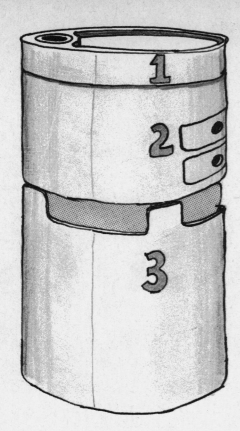

ALUMINUM or STEEL PIPE *

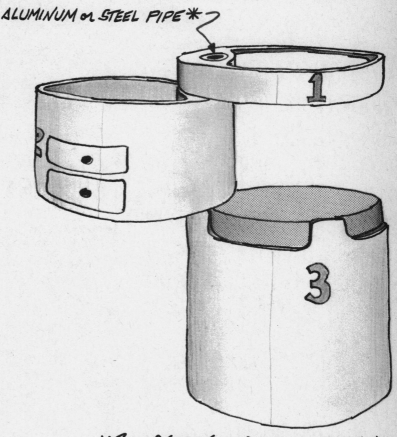

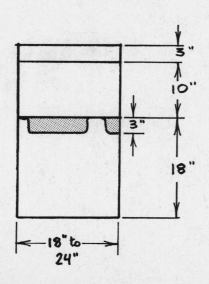

UPHOLSTER THE SEAT IN FOAM & PAINT THE UNIT [or USE BRIGHT CONTACT PAPER or FABRIC TO COVER THEM].

*LEAD or HEAVY PVC PIPE MAY BE USED FOR THE CHILDREN'S VERSION.

JIM DESIGNED & BUILT THIS PLYWOOD & ROPE TREE-HOUSE for HIS SON MIKE. IT'S A TRULY NOMADIC STRUCTURE. IT ASSEMBLES & KNOCKS DOWN EASILY & TAKES UP LITTLE SPACE WHEN APART. ➡ HANG IT FROM A TREE or THE EAVES of YOUR ROOF, OR EVEN FROM AN EXISTING SWING SET. ➡ ROPE USED IS ½" Ø SISAL, WHICH IS VERY CHEAP; ON THE LADDER ⅜" Ø NYLON ROPE WAS USED.

(96)

Note: THE ¾" THICK PLYWOOD DISK CAN BE BOUGHT PRECUT TO A 48" CIRCLE, BUT THIS COSTS NEARLY AS MUCH AS A FULL SHEET & PLYWOOD. WE SUGGEST YOU FIND A FRIEND & BUY A FULL SHEET & MAKE 2 HOUSES. THE WHOLE TREE-HOUSE IS TETHERED FOR STABILITY. ➡ START THE TREE-HOUSE LOW TO THE GROUND. AS THE KIDS GROW, RAISE IT! PRESERVE THE WOOD WITH PAINT OR VARNISH.

CUT-OUT PATTERN
FOR 48" DIAM., ¾"
PLYWOOD PLATFORM
SET:

THE LADDER IS MADE OF
12" LENGTHS OF 2"×2" PINE.
DRILL NEAR EACH
END FOR A ⅜" ROPE.

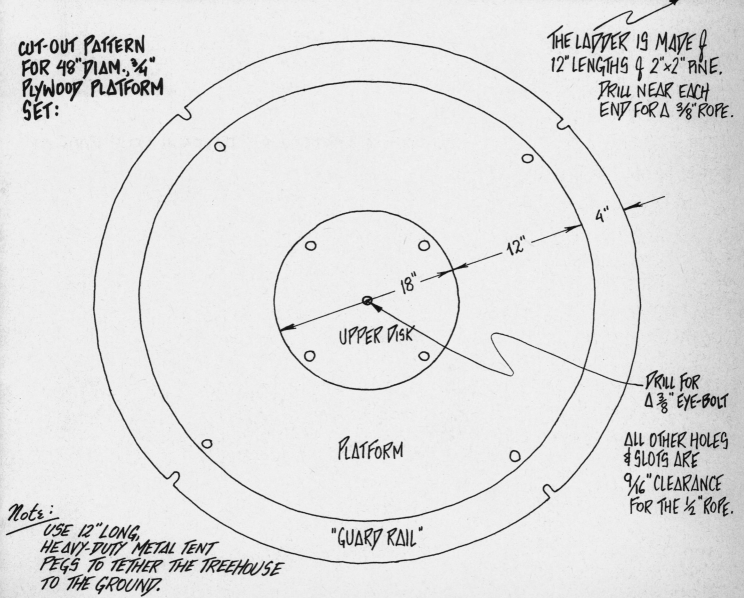

18"

12"

4"

UPPER DISK

DRILL FOR
A ⅜" EYE-BOLT

PLATFORM

ALL OTHER HOLES
& SLOTS ARE
9/16" CLEARANCE
FOR THE ½" ROPE.

"GUARD RAIL"

Note:
USE 12" LONG,
HEAVY-DUTY METAL TENT
PEGS TO TETHER THE TREEHOUSE
TO THE GROUND.

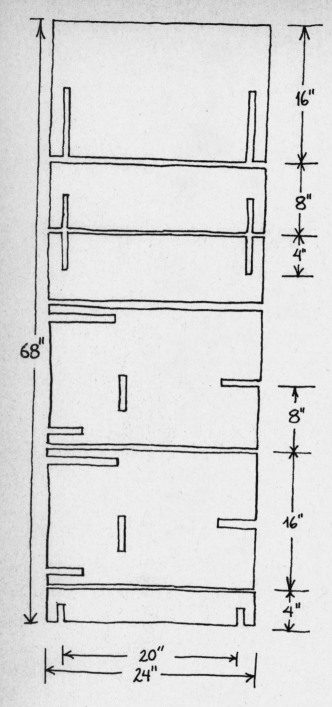

16"

8"

4"

68"

8"

16"

4"

20"

24"

SIMPLE WORK TABLE & SEAT FOR CHILDREN:

AS YOU SEE, YOU CAN GET THE WHOLE UNIT OUT OF ½ A SHEET OF CHIPBOARD, PARTICLE BOARD OR ¾" PLY. IN OTHER WORDS: TWO OF THESE TABLES OUT OF ONE SHEET, WITH A PIECE 2×4

FEET LEFT OVER. BY CUTTING SLITS CAREFULLY, YOU CAN JUST "SWEAT-FIT" IT TOGETHER, OR ELSE GLUE IT. FINISH NATURALLY OR PAINT IN POP COLOURS AND ADD CASTERS.

KEN YOST HAS DEVELOPED A NUMBER OF BEAUTIFULLY CRAFTED FURNITURE PIECES, ONE OF THEM THIS CRIB FOR HIS SON ERIC. WHEN ERIC WAS A BABY, THE CRIB WAS UPSIDE DOWN, PROVIDING A HIGHER & MORE EASILY ACCESSIBLE SURFACE. BY MAKING IT A DOUBLE~FUNCTION PIECE, KEN HAS PROLONGED THE USEFUL LIFE OF THE CRIB AND HAS ELIMINATED THE NEED TO DISPOSE OF A USEFUL PIECE OF FURNITURE.

≫ TO DEFINE IS TO KILL, TO SUGGEST
IS TO CREATE. ≪
MALLARMÉ

EATING· WORKING· SLEEPING· LOUNGING:

TO DEFINE, THEN, AND TO MAKE EXPEDIENT CLASSIFICATIONS INTO SEPARATE AREAS IS NOT POSSIBLE WITH MUCH of THE FURNITURE IN THIS SECTION. NOT BECAUSE THE MATTRESS ROLL-UPS, SAY, WOULD WORK EQUALLY WELL IN SLEEPING, LOUNGING or EATING SITUATIONS, OR BECAUSE THE ROLLING TABLE MIGHT EASILY BE AN OUTDOOR or INDOOR WORK AID, AN EATING SURFACE or A BAR. RATHER WE ARE STILL LOOKING AT THE SITU-ATION UPSIDE DOWN. IT IS THE

NATURE OF THESE ACTIVITIES THEMSELVES THAT HAS CHANGED.

THE DIVIDING LINE BETWEEN WHAT IS "WORK" AND WHAT IS "LEISURE" HAS LOST SOME OF ITS MEANING FOR MANY OF US.

THE STRICT UPRIGHT, UPTIGHT SITTING POSTURE OF GREAT-GRANDFATHER'S TIME HAS BECOME A SPRAWL, A RELAXED LOUNGING POSTURE AKIN TO SLEEP.

WHAT IS OUR TWO-LEVEL "FUN-SPACE" IF NOT AN ENVIRONMENTAL STRUCTURE IN WHICH TO SLEEP, LOUNGE, TALK, WORK, EAT, LOVE?

TO DESIGN MEANS, AMONG OTHER THINGS, TO HAVE ONE FOOT IN THE FUTURE, TO ANTICIPATE: OUR IDEAS IN THIS BOOK TRY TO ANTICIPATE HOW YOU MAY WISH TO LIVE IN THAT FUTURE, AND TRY TO PROVIDE YOU WITH REASONABLE NOTIONS FROM WHICH TO START YOUR OWN WORK OF CONSTRUCTING YOUR OWN ENVIRONMENT.

OUR HOPE IS THAT THESE PAGES ARE BRIDGES BETWEEN YOUR WISHES AND THE REAL WORLD.

SIMPLEST FOLDING TRAY TABLE:

JENNIFER SATU AT 3 CAN EASILY HANDLE ONE OF THESE.

THE BOTTOM [WHEN ERECTED] IS 18" TALL & MADE OF ⑫ ½" ⌀ DOWELS WITH ④ 1½" ⌀ DOWELS DRILLED INTO & SERVING AS ENDS. THIS IS HELD TOGETHER BY A 12" STOVE BOLT WITH A CROWN-NUT AT EITHER END, THIS BEING ALSO THE SWIVEL & FOLDING ACTION.

THE TRAY [OR TABLE TOP] IS MADE OF SMALL END-GRAIN SQUARES OF TEAK, GLUED INTO A BUTCHER BLOCK [17½" × 17½" × 1" THICK].*

A ROUND KERF-CUT HOLDS THE BASE IN PLACE AT EACH END. TO KEEP THE BASE FROM OPENING TOO FAR, A 2" WIDE PLASTIC STRAP IS STAPLED ON [SEE TOP PHOTO]

* SEE: NOMADIC FURNITURE 1, p.53, FOR HOW TO MAKE A BUTCHER BLOCK.

MATTRESS ROLL-UPS & FOLD-UPS:

THERE ARE LOTS of WAYS of COMBINING SITTING & LYING UNITS, USING FOAM. THIS UNIT IS MADE of 3" THICK FOAM, 24" WIDE & 10 FEET LONG! EITHER ADULTS or CHILDREN CAN SLOUCH, SPRAWL, SIT or SLEEP on IT [WHEN PARTIALLY UNROLLED]. IT IS CANVAS-COVERED & HELD IN ITS ROLLED POSITION BY TIES.

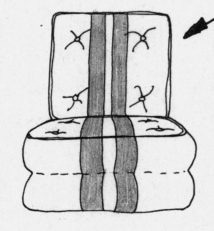

THIS FOLD-UP 3-POSITION UNIT IS MADE of 3 PIECES of FOAM, EACH 26"x26" & 3" THICK. IN COVERING ALL THREE IN COTTON or CANVAS, SEW THE COVER SO IT BECOMES ITS OWN HINGE [SEE 3RD DRAWING]. TO MAKE IT SERVE AS A CHAIR, LEAN IT AGAINST A WALL.

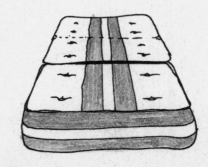

FOLDING TRAY TABLE:

THIS IS EVEN SIMPLER THAN IT LOOKS:

1/ MAKE 3 IDENTICAL OPEN HARDWOOD FRAMES OUT OF 1"× 1" LUMBER & PUT THEM TOGETHER WITH 2 PIANO HINGES TO MAKE THE OPEN "SCREEN".

[10"×24" EACH IS ONE OF MANY POSSIBLE SIZES].

2/ MAKE ANOTHER FRAME, BUT WITH A ¼" PLYWOOD TOP. BE SURE THAT THE FRAME HAS A LIP [AS SHOWN IN DETAIL].

15"× 30" MIGHT BE A DECENT SIZE.

*

Both parts are flat & take up little room :

the top can serve as a tray alone. Several are handy for a lap-supper.

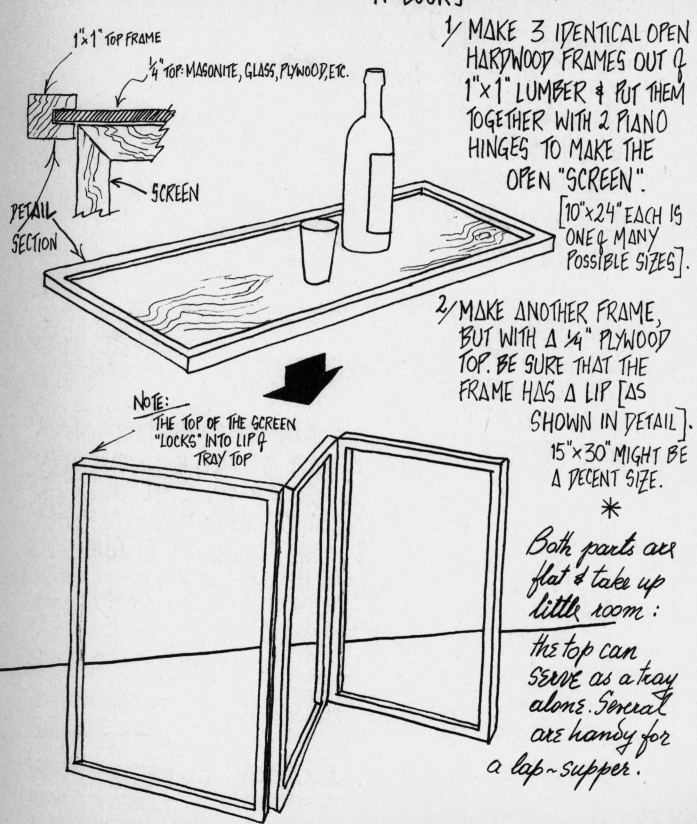

1"×1" TOP FRAME

¼" TOP: MASONITE, GLASS, PLYWOOD, ETC.

SCREEN

DETAIL SECTION

NOTE:
THE TOP OF THE SCREEN "LOCKS" INTO LIP OF TRAY TOP

ONE OF THE MOST ELEGANT IDEAS IN THE BOOK: A SMALL TABLE THAT ROLLS UP & TUCKS AWAY & IS STILL STURDY. A RUBBER THONG HOLDS THE BEECH SLATS IN TENSION, LEGS SCREW IN TO STABILIZE IT ALL.

THE TABLE IS 20" TALL, TOP IS ROUGHLY 20" x 20". IT OPENS THE WAY TO OTHER, LARGER STRUCTURES, DEVELOPING THE PRINCIPLE FURTHER...

DESIGNED BY AXEL THYGESEN,

➤ INTERNA, COPENHAGEN, DENMARK.

FOLDING SERVICE CART:

THIS ONE REALLY FOLDS FLAT & COULD HANG IN A CLOSET or THE GARAGE. USES?

DIAPERS & BABY THINGS, BARBEQUE STUFF, GARDENING THINGS, DRINKS & A PATIO SNACK, TOOLS & WORK SUPPLIES, SEWING & CRAFT MATERIALS, + ALL THE HUNDREDS of THINGS YOU'LL THINK UP!

THE CART CAN BE MADE of $\frac{1}{2}$" or $\frac{3}{4}$" PLYWOOD, BUT NOTE THAT ➡ WHEELS MUST BE MADE of $\frac{3}{4}$" PLY. IF YOU WISH YOU CAN EDGE THE WHEELS WITH RUBBER STRIPS TO INCREASE FRICTION.

➡ A CLEAR BAR-TOP VARNISH WILL KEEP THE TABLE TOP IN GOOD SHAPE.

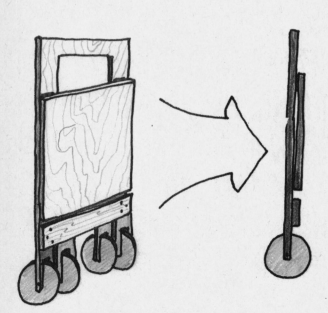

LEG SUPPORT Ⓐ

7 7/8"

HINGES ARE BUTT UP TO THIS LINE

ASSEMBLY DIAGRAM

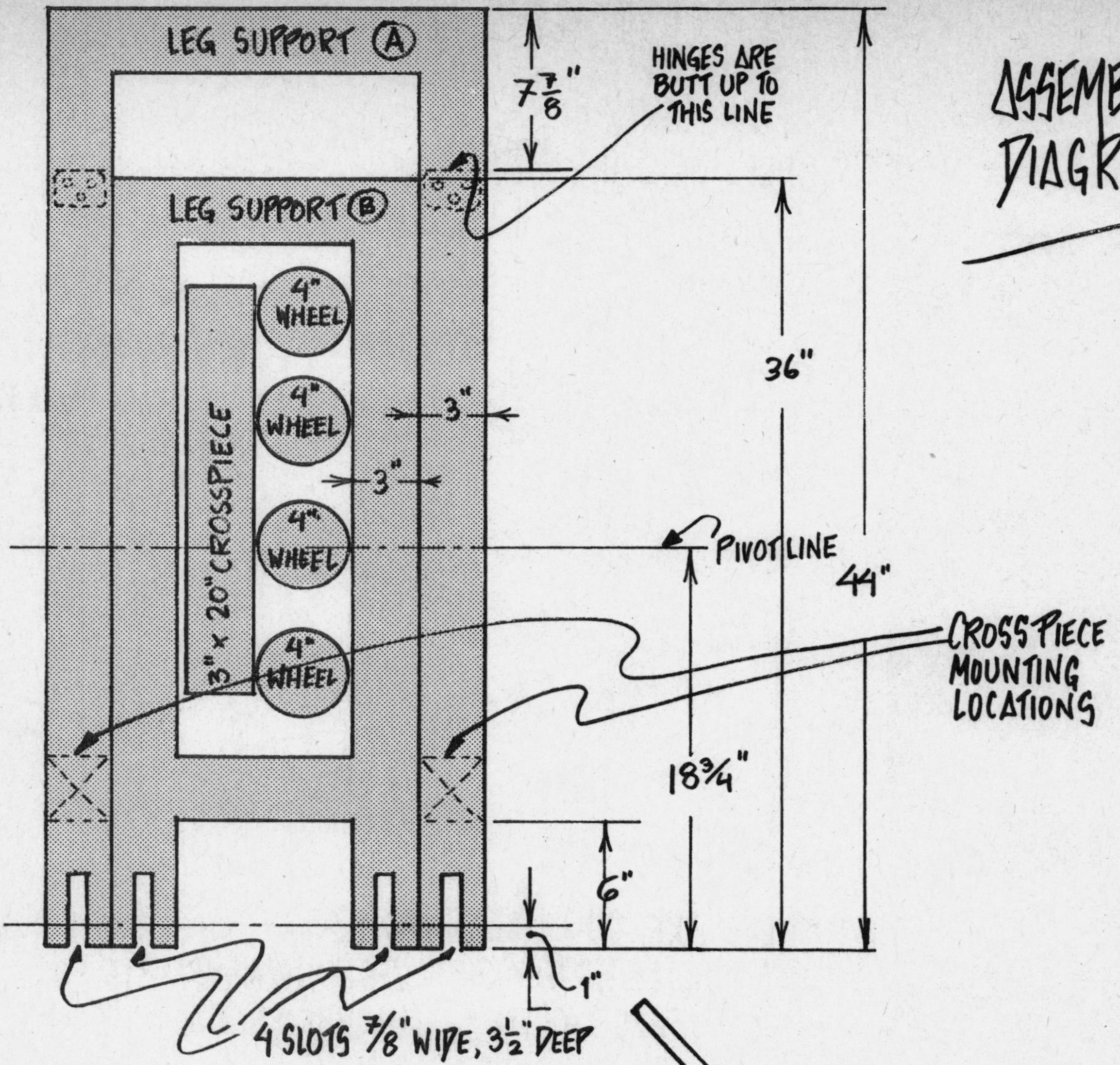

LEG SUPPORT Ⓑ

4" WHEEL

4" WHEEL

3"

3"

4" WHEEL

36"

3" x 20" CROSSPIECE

4" WHEEL

PIVOT LINE

44"

CROSS PIECE MOUNTING LOCATIONS

18 3/4"

6"

1"

4 SLOTS 7/8" WIDE, 3 1/2" DEEP

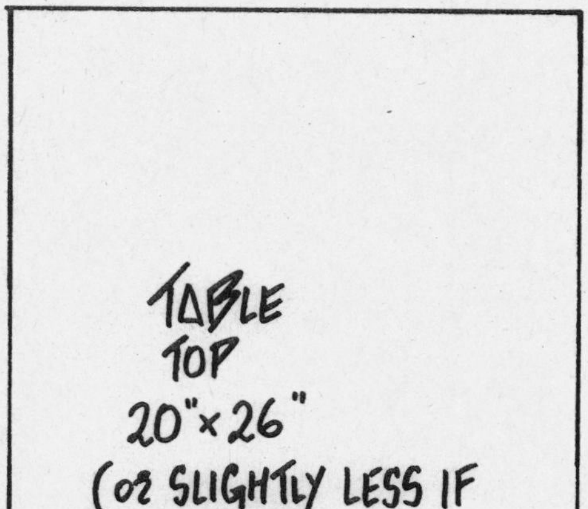

TABLE TOP
20" x 26"
(OR SLIGHTLY LESS IF EDGED)

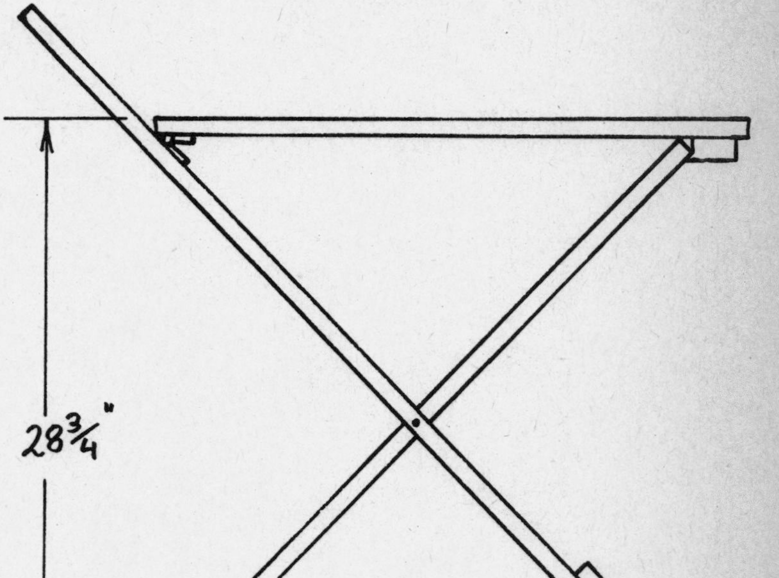

28 3/4"

108

JIM'S PEG-LOCK

JIM ORIGINALLY DEVELOPED THIS LOCKING SYSTEM FOR A BABY~CRIB* IN OUR EARLIER BOOK. WE BOTH THOUGHT IT WAS INTERESTING ENOUGH TO PRESENT IT AGAIN WITH SOME NEW IDEAS FOR ITS USE.

TOTALLY KNOCK-DOWN END/SERVICE TABLE.

THERE ARE COUNTLESS OTHER POSSIBILITIES: BOOKSHELVES, UNDERSUPPORTS FOR TABLES, BEDS & COUCHES - CHILDREN'S PLAY HOUSES - FUN-CUBES AND MANY, MANY MORE.

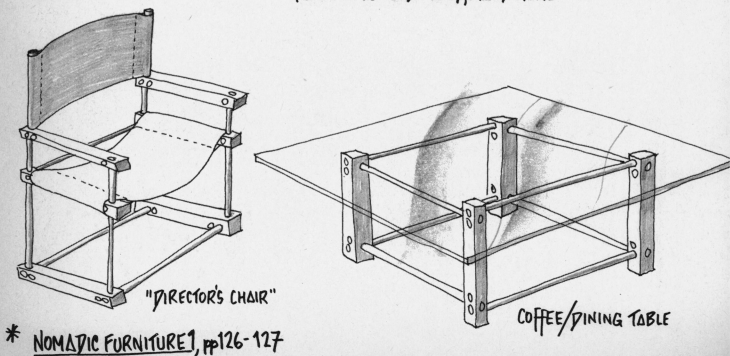

"DIRECTOR'S CHAIR"

COFFEE/DINING TABLE

* <u>NOMADIC FURNITURE 1</u>, pp 126-127

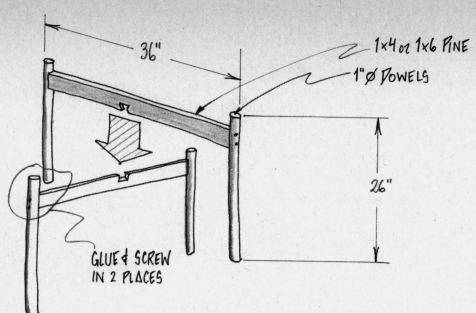

36"

1x4 or 1x6 PINE

1"∅ DOWELS

26"

GLUE & SCREW
IN 2 PLACES

THESE SIZES MAY BE CHANGED
TO SUIT YOUR INDIVIDUAL NEEDS.
THE 3/4" PLYWOOD TABLE TOPS
ARE AVAILABLE AT MOST
LUMBER YARDS, AND RANGE
FROM 12" DIAMETER STOOL TOPS
TO 48" TABLE TOPS.

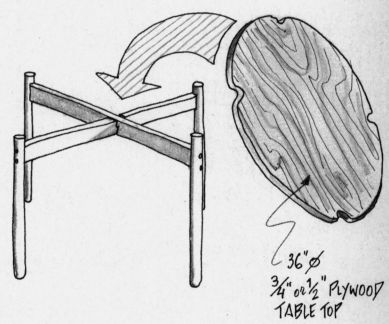

36" ∅
3/4" or 1/2" PLYWOOD
TABLE TOP

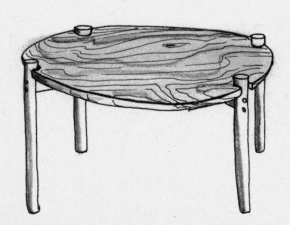

SIMPLE TAKE~APART TABLE:

SYSTEM ABSTRACTA
DESIGNED BY POUL CADOVIUS

THIS IS PROBABLY THE MOST FLEXIBLE OF ALL THE MANY SYSTEMS THAT DEPEND ON A SERIES OF CONNECTORS, RODS & SHELVING PIECES.

THIS CONNECTOR IS THE HEART OF THE SYSTEM. BESIDES THIS 6-WAY NODE SHOWN, IT ALSO COMES WITH ONLY 2, 3, 4 or 5 TERMINALS, DEPENDING ON ITS USE IN THE STRUCTURE. THE RODS COME IN 15 LENGTHS FROM 65mm (2½") TO 805mm (31¾") & ARE CHROMED. THE RODS POP EASILY INTO THE CONNECTORS. METAL, WOOD & GLASS SHELVING ARE AVAILABLE AS ARE VINYL-DIPPED HANGING TRAY-BASKETS FOR MAGAZINES, KNITTING, TOYS or WHATHAVEYOU. ALL SHELVING & TRAYS CLIP INTO THE STRUCTURE.

AN INFINITE NUMBER of COMBINATIONS — FROM A GLASS-TOPPED
COFFEE TABLE on CASTERS [THEY HAVE THOSE TOO, AS WELL AS CLIP-ON LIGHTS],
TO BOOKCASES, A STORAGE WALL or EXHIBITION STRUCTURES-ARE POSSIBLE.
TAGE SCHMIDT IN FREDENSBORG HAS A STORAGE WALL FOR HI-FI, BOOKS,
TAPES, RECORDS, ETC. → THE PRICE IS COMPARABLE TO SIMILAR UNITS
IN WOOD. ABSTRACTA, HOWEVER, IS HIGHLY NOMADIC & WILL GROW or
SHRINK AS YOUR NEEDS DO. THE SYSTEM IS PATENTED & HERE ARE
SOME DISTRIBUTORS:

↓

ABSTRACTA STRUCTURES INC.
101 PARK AVENUE
NEW YORK 10017, USA

↓

WARSHAW LTD.
NETIL HOUSE
1-7 WESTGATE ST.
LONDON, ENGLAND

↓

CADO-ABSTRACTA
H.C. ØRSTEDSVEJ 45
1879 COPENHAGEN V.
DENMARK

FLAT~FOLDING TABLE:

A SMALL, INEXPENSIVE YUGOSLAVIAN* FLAT-FOLDING CHAIR INSPIRED US TO DESIGN A TABLE BASED ON THIS HIGHLY PORTABLE & STACKABLE FORMAT.

OUR VERSION OF SUCH A TABLE WAS MADE OF ½" FINNISH PLYWOOD & ENTIRELY ROUTED. IT COULD ALSO BE MADE OF AMERICAN PLYWOOD, UP TO ¾" & THE SHAPES BE CUT OUT WITH A SABRE SAW. WHEN FOLDED, OUR TABLE WAS 30"×39" AND JUST ONE INCH THICK.

➡ TO CONSTRUCT THE TABLE, MAKE ONE EACH OF DIAGRAM Ⓐ & Ⓑ. NOTE THAT THE UNDER-TABLE FRAME IS DERIVED FROM DIAGRAM Ⓑ. THE TABLE TOP IS FIXED TO THE A-FRAME LEG STRUCTURE THROUGH THIS FRAME. WE USED 6" LONG EYE-BOLTS FOR LOCKING THE TABLE TOP INTO AN UPRIGHT POSITION. THEY WERE LOCATED AT POINT "X" IN THE SIDE VIEW ON THE NEXT PAGE.

6" LONG GALVANIZED GUTTER NAILS WERE USED FOR THE PIVOT POINT AND WERE DRIVEN FROM INSIDE THE FRAME TOWARD THE OUTER LEG EDGE.

* U.S. PRICE, AUTUMN 1973, WAS $8.88 PER CHAIR AT SAFEWAY DISCOUNT DRUG STORES, IN WHITE, BLACK, RED or WALNUT-STAINED.

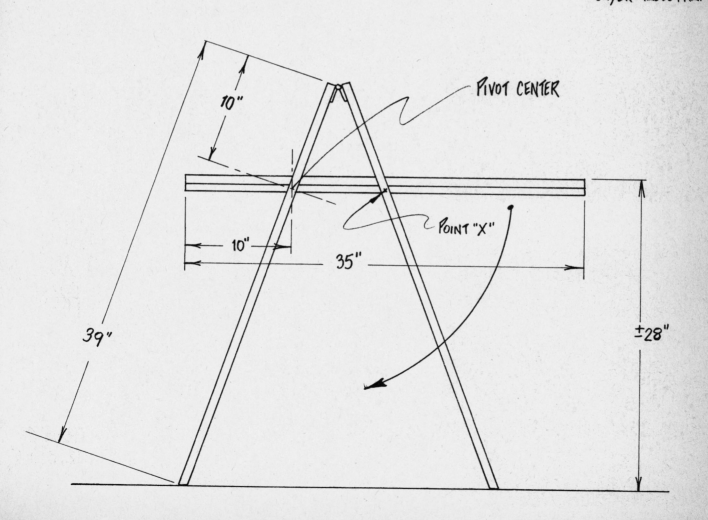

3" 24" 3"

3" 24" 3"
3" 18" 3"

39"

REMOVE
SCRAP
PANEL

4"   4"

30"   30"

DIAGRAM (A)   TABLE TOP   DIAGRAM (B)   UNDER-TABLE FRAME

10"

PIVOT CENTER

10"   POINT "X"

35"

39"

±28"

PUT A PHOTO OR
POSTER HERE

FOLD~DOWN DESKS

JIM DESIGNED THESE
SIMPLE FOLD~DOWN DESKS
FOR USE IN REALLY CRAMPED
QUARTERS. AS YOU CAN SEE,
THEY FOLD FLAT TO THE WALL
WHEN NOT IN USE. THE
LARGER ONE WOULD BE
NO THICKER THAN AN INCH
[IF USING 1/2" PLYWOOD OR
PRESSBOARD]. USE A LENGTH
OF PLUMBER'S CHAIN TO KEEP
THE LEG STABLE.

CHAIN

BULLETIN
BOARD

THIS "SIMPLEST" VERSION CAN BE CUT
FROM A SINGLE SHEET WITH A SABRE SAW
AND SCROLL-CUTTING BLADE. IT CAN FOLD
INTO ITSELF TO BECOME ITS ORIGINAL
THICKNESS. DON'T USE THE CHAIN ON
THIS VERSION, AS IT WOULD PREVENT
THE DESK FROM FOLDING. MOUNT
A PEGBOARD, BULLETIN BOARD, ETC.
TO THE FRONT OF THE LEG UNIT. TO
SECURE THE LEG, ATTACH EITHER
RUBBER FEET FOR A SMOOTH
FLOOR OR "TACK STRIP" FOR A
CARPETED FLOOR.

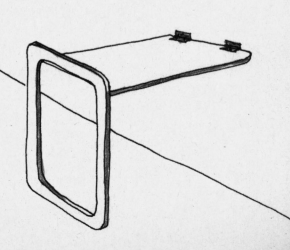

COUCH~BED CONCEPT:

THIS ARRANGEMENT WAS DESIGNED BY JIM TO BE "MOST FOR LEAST". ITS CONSTRUCTION SHOULD BE EASY ENOUGH FOR ANYONE TO ACHIEVE.

➡ THE MAIN ADVANTAGE IN THIS CONCEPT [BESIDES EASE & LOCATING THE PARTS] IS THAT THE COUCH IS SELF-SUPPORTING & DOESN'T NEED TO BE PLACED AGAINST A WALL.

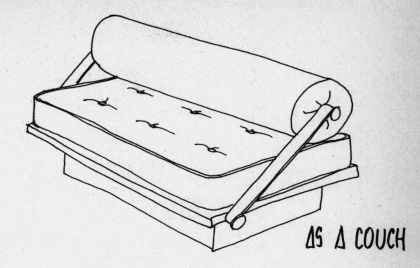

AS A COUCH

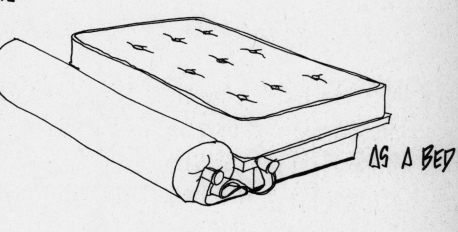

AS A BED

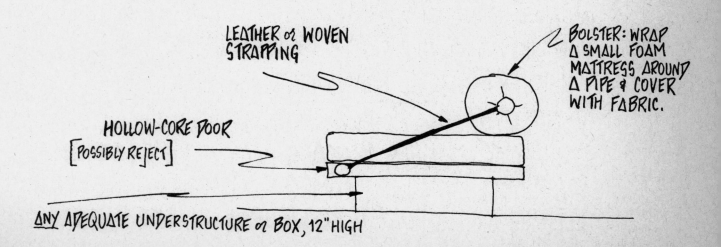

LEATHER or WOVEN STRAPPING

BOLSTER: WRAP A SMALL FOAM MATTRESS AROUND A PIPE & COVER WITH FABRIC.

HOLLOW-CORE DOOR [POSSIBLY REJECT]

ANY ADEQUATE UNDERSTRUCTURE or BOX, 12" HIGH

SPACE DIVIDERS

THERE ARE AN INFINITE NUMBER of WAYS YOU CAN DEVELOP TO DIVIDE ROOMS, SCREEN AREAS OFF VISUALLY or CREATE NEW SPACES FOR SPECIAL FUNCTIONS. SINCE YOU'RE WORKING <u>INSIDE</u> A HOME or STUDIO YOU CAN USE SUCH FRAGILE MATERIALS AS JAPANESE RICE PAPERS [SHOJI], CHINESE SILKS or GLUED-TOGETHER SLICES of CARDBOARD MAILING TUBES TO CREATE DELIGHT.

• SINCE THIS WHOLE BOOK IS <u>NOT</u> A DO-IT-YOURSELF GUIDE, BUT RATHER A MEANS TO GET YOUR OWN THOUGHTS & FEELINGS GOING IN YOUR OWN ENVIRONMENT, WE ONLY SHOW TWO SIMPLE VERSIONS TO GET YOU STARTED.

• THE <u>FREE-STANDING ADD-ON CLOSET</u> IS SHOWN IN A SKETCH & PLAN VIEW ON THE RIGHT. IT'S MADE of VARIOUS HOLLOW-CORE DOORS THAT ARE HINGED TOGETHER. THIS WILL MAKE IT FREESTANDING, EASILY PUT UP & EASILY MOVED. THE CLOTHES RACK [1"∅ STEEL PIPE, SHOWN IN THE PLAN ONLY] ADDS STABILITY. WITH THIS SYSTEM YOU CAN ADD A CLOSET, WORKSHOP or OFFICE TO AN EXISTING ROOM. ➡ FIGURE OUT THE SPACE YOU NEED & DEVELOP YOUR OWN SYSTEM.

• THE <u>FREE-STANDING DIVIDER</u> [PHOTO] WAS DE~ VELOPED BY TIM PETERSON & CHRIS GLUCK, TWO CALARTS STUDENTS. IT USES 3"∅ ABS PLASTIC PIPE [THE CHEAPEST AVAILABLE] FOR THE FRAMES. PANELS ARE CANVAS. THE CLAMPS ARE LAMINATED PLYWOOD. ➡ WHY NOT POCKETS ON THE CANVAS PANELS?

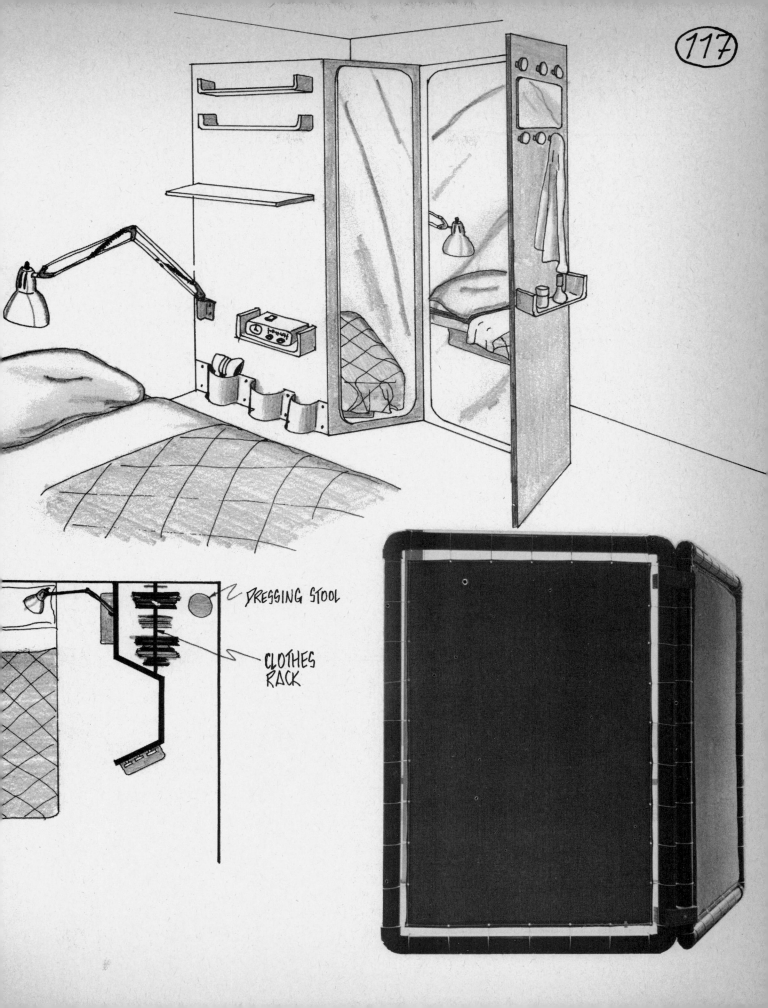

DRESSING STOOL

CLOTHES RACK

WORK & STORAGE CENTER:

THIS CAN BE BUILT OUT of ¾" PLYWOOD, FINNPLY or PARTICLE BOARD. AS YOU SEE, IT CONSISTS of 2 UNITS THAT ARE OF IDENTICAL SIZE BUT DIFFER IN INTERIOR SHELVING ARRANGEMENTS. BOTH UNITS SIT ON CASTERS; THE THIRD UNIT IS AN "OVER-TABLE" THAT WILL STORE THE TWO UNITS, OR HIDE THEM or SERVE AS A SIDE DESK. WE HAVE NOT GIVEN SPECIFIC DIMENSIONS AS THESE ARE APT TO DIFFER, DEPENDING ON YOUR SEWING MACHINE, TYPEWRITER, FILES, ETC.

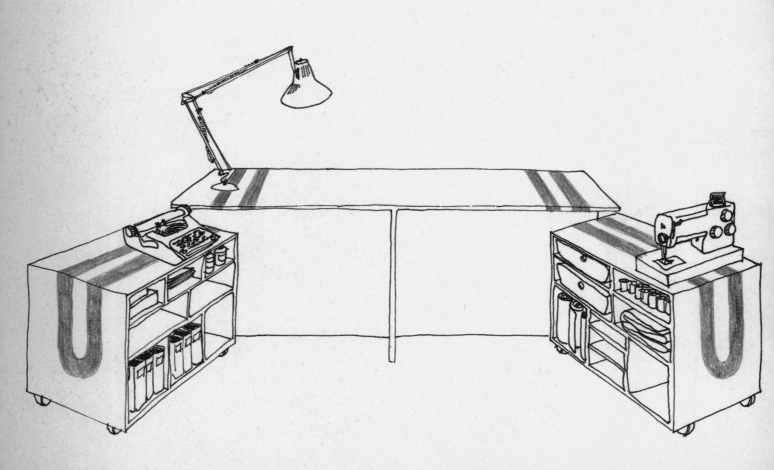

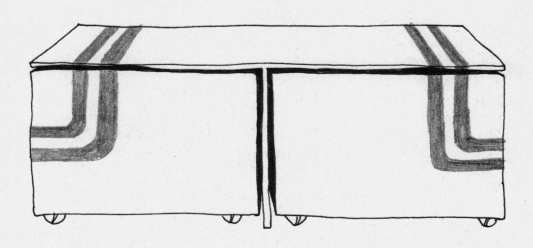

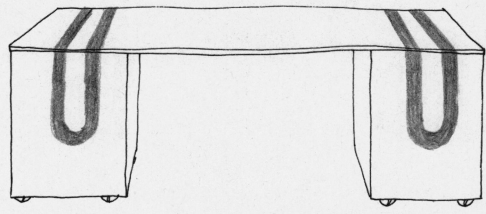

Note: THE "OVER-TABLE" IS A GREAT CUTTING AREA FOR SEWING.

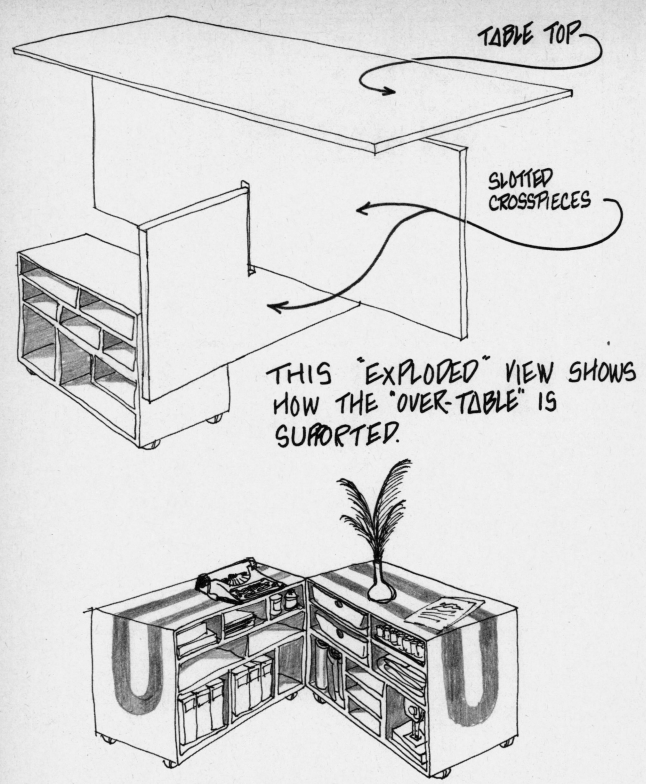

TABLE TOP

SLOTTED CROSSPIECES

THIS "EXPLODED" VIEW SHOWS HOW THE "OVER-TABLE" IS SUPPORTED.

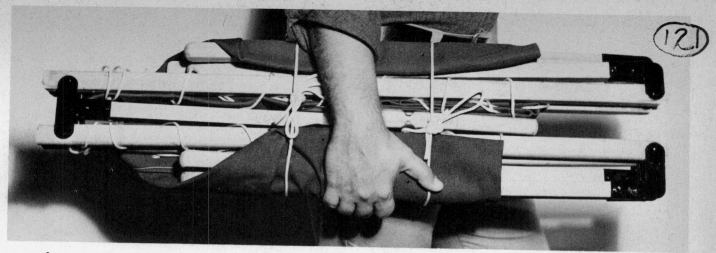

STILL ONE OF THE GREATEST NOMADIC DESIGNS AROUND, THIS ARMY COT WAS RETRIEVED FOR $3.- FROM A GARAGE SALE.

SINCE THE ORIGINAL COVER WAS DIRTY & DRAB, BILL MANNS SEWED UP A NEW ONE FOR JIM IN HEAVY CANVAS.

THE RESULT WAS MORE COMFORTABLE & BETTER-LOOKING THAN EXPECTED. THIS MAKES A GOOD EXTRA BED WHEN FRIENDS COME BY TO CRASH.

ABITACOLO*
DESIGNED BY
BRUNO
MUNARI

(122)

THIS IS THE "HIGH-TECHNOLOGY" EQUIVALENT &
OUR 4 PAGES & CUBES IN THE EARLIER BOOK.
THIS IS THE WAY IT LOOKS ON ARRIVAL & IT EXTENDS
*ABITACOLO MEANS "COCKPIT"   TO THIS.

THIS FUNKY ITALIAN IMPORT WEIGHS 110 lbs, IS MADE of STEEL THAT HAS BEEN EPOXY~RESIN-CLAD. THE COLOUR IS "A PALE GRAY, TO GO WITH EVERYTHING," WE ARE TOLD. IT WILL ALSO "SUPPORT AS MANY AS 20 PEOPLE." THESE TWENTY MUST BE THE MANUFACTURERS...

WHY ELSE WOULD 20 PEOPLE CRAWL INTO A BUNK-BED WITH GLORIFIED (?) HEADBOARDS?

A WASTE of STEEL & RESINS TO MAKE A RICH MAN'S JUNGLE-GYM, BUT SOME GOOD STRUCTURAL DESIGN.

⇨ ROBOTS MILANO VIALE CALDARA 34 MILAN, ITALY

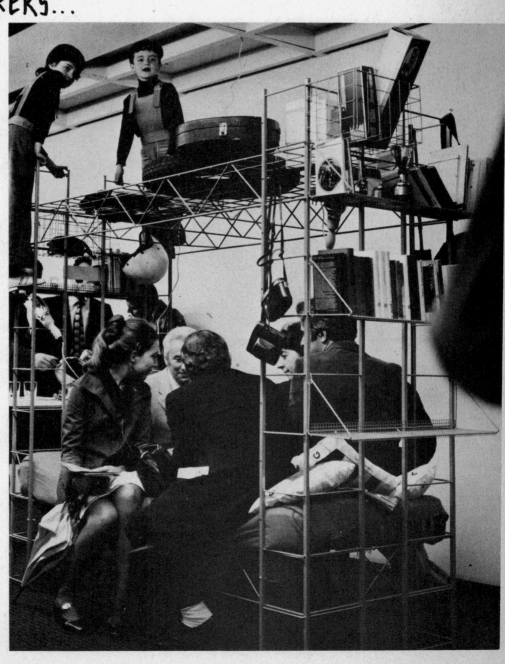

TWO-LEVEL FUN-SPACE (CONVERSION):

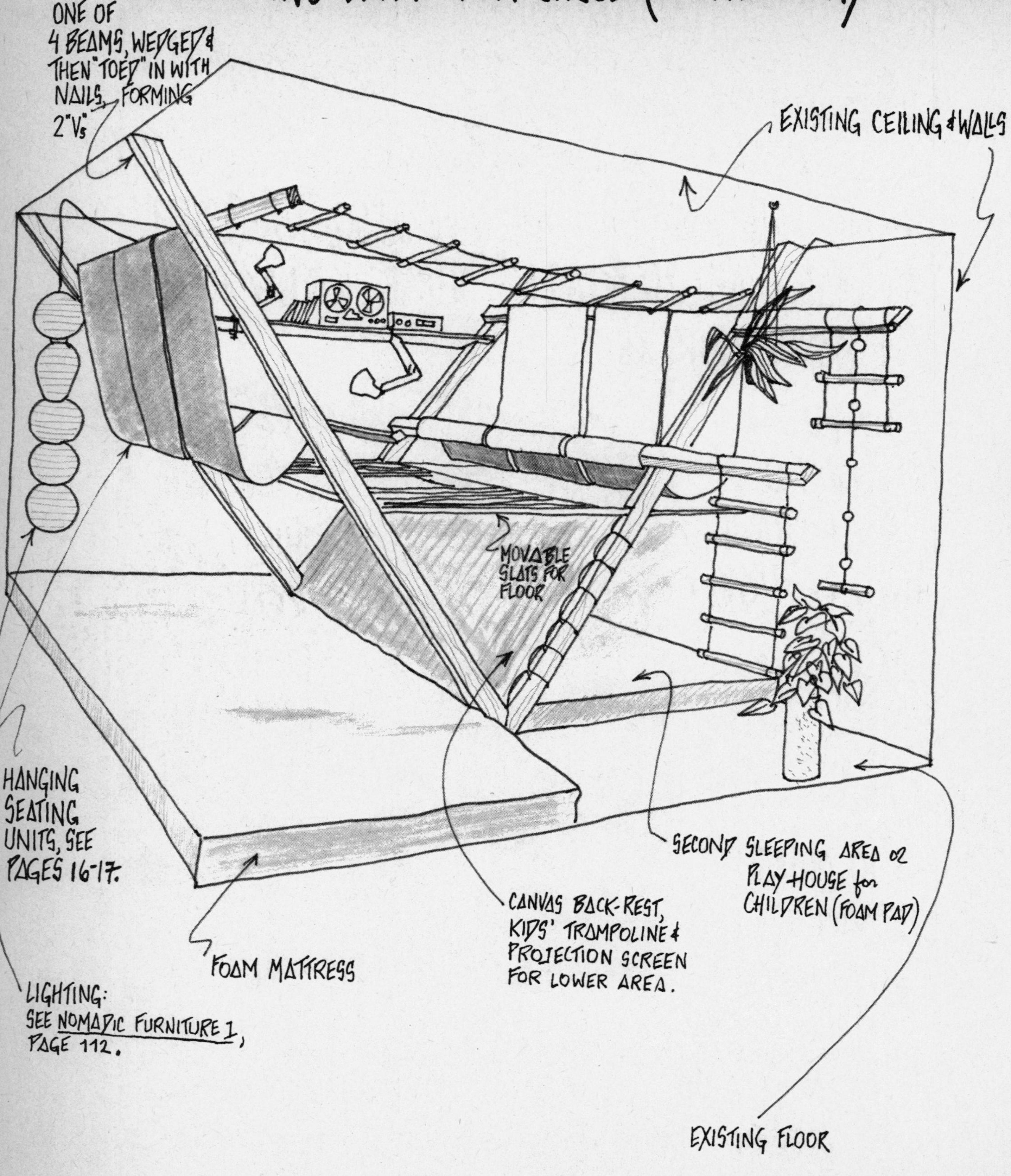

ONE OF
4 BEAMS, WEDGED &
THEN "TOED" IN WITH
NAILS, FORMING
2" "V"s

EXISTING CEILING & WALLS

MOVABLE
SLATS FOR
FLOOR

HANGING
SEATING
UNITS, SEE
PAGES 16-17.

SECOND SLEEPING AREA or
PLAY-HOUSE for
CHILDREN (FOAM PAD)

CANVAS BACK-REST,
KIDS' TRAMPOLINE &
PROJECTION SCREEN
FOR LOWER AREA.

FOAM MATTRESS

LIGHTING:
SEE NOMADIC FURNITURE 1,
PAGE 112.

EXISTING FLOOR

WE HAVE GIVEN NO SIZES FOR THIS FUN-SPACE SINCE IT ALL DEPENDS ON HOW MUCH of A ROOM or ATTIC YOU'LL WANT TO USE. OBVIOUSLY THE HEIGHT of THE TOTAL SPACE SHOULD BE <u>MINIMALLY</u> 8 FEET!

THE 4 BEAMS FORMING THE TWO "V's" AT EITHER END SHOULD BE AT LEAST 3"x6". 4"x8" MAKES MORE SENSE.

VIC [IN HIS FORTIES] CAN CLAMBER AROUND A SPACE LIKE THIS, BUT DON'T EXPECT TO HAVE GRANDMA or YOUR IN-LAWS RELAX IN THIS GOOFY JUNGLE~GYM! IT'S GREAT for CHILDREN AND CATS, AND, GENERALLY SPEAKING, FREE SOULS UNDER 35. DON'T JUST BUILD IT. CHANGE IT AND MAKE IT BETTER!

1/ CUT BEAMS TO LENGTHS NEEDED.
2/ CUT OUT 3 PLACES ON EACH BEAM. TWO FOR SEATING AND ONE FOR THE SLATS OR DOWELS THAT WILL BE BOTH MOVABLE FLOOR & ACCESS HOLE.
3/ PEG BEAMS ATTACH AT BOTTOM of "V's" WITH 1" DOWEL or CARRIAGE BOLT.
4/ WEDGE THE "V's" INTO PLACE & [IF NEEDED] "TOE" IN WITH NAILS AGAINST CEILING & FLOOR.
5/ ATTACH SEATING, SLAT "FLOOR", ROPE LADDERS, SHELVING, WHATEVER.
6/ HAVE FUN!

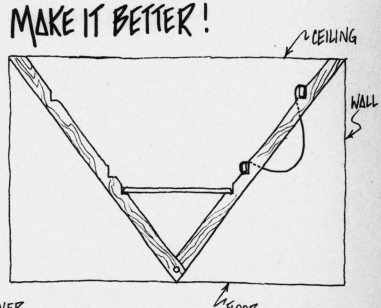

BILL MANNS, ONE OF JIM'S STUDENTS, CAN SERVE AS A GOOD EXAMPLE OF THE NOMADIC COLLEGE STUDENT. HIS APARTMENT IS WARM [COSY, GEMÜTLICH, HYGGELIG], AND INVITINGLY SPEAKS OF HIS PERSONAL DESIGN TASTE. IT WAS INCREDIBLY INEXPENSIVE TO CREATE. LIKE JIM HE WORKS WITH THE CONCEPT OF "THE MOST FOR THE LEAST" — LIKE VIC HE FEELS THAT IN 1973/74 LESS IS MORE.

THE SLING COUCH ABOVE COST A TOTAL OF $17.50 AND WILL CONVERT TO A BED BY DROPPING DOWN THE BACK SUPPORT. HE USED 20 FT. OF TUBING → $6.50, $6.00 WORTH OF CANVAS AND 4"×4" PINE LENGTHS AMOUNTING TO $5.00. ➡ SIZE OF THE SLING COUCH IS 30"×30"; ENTIRE UNIT IS 78" LONG.

BILL'S BOOKSHELF IS A STUDY IN PRACTICAL THINKING. IT IS MADE OF "PECKY CEDAR", POSSIBLY THE CHEAPEST AVAILABLE. HE PAID $1⁰⁰ EACH for THE 1"×12"×72" BOARDS. HE NAILED THEM TOGETHER AND ADDED A DIAGONAL CROSSPIECE for STABILITY. TOTAL COST: $7⁰⁰

P.S.: THE UNIT WAS PLACED <u>IN FRONT</u> of A WINDOW, GIVING A VERY PLEASANT EFFECT & CUTTING DOWN ON HEATING COSTS.

127

THESE REFLECTORS [ALUMINUM], WERE FOUND IN A SURPLUS STORE AT 25¢ EACH.

THE UPPER UNIT HAS A LAMP MOUNTED IN IT. A PLEXIGLASS CIRCLE WAS PLACED ON THE BOTTOM UNIT, WHICH IS FILLED WITH DRIED WEEDS.

BOTH ILLUMINATION & GENERAL APPEARANCE ARE GREAT.

more about cubes:

MANY OF US HAVE FOUND THAT CUBES ARE TERRIFIC GENERAL-PURPOSE DEVICES. THEY CAN BECOME TABLES, TABLE SUPPORTS, DESK OR BED SUPPORTS, SHIPPING & MOVING CRATES, PLAY~BOXES, SCULPTURE BASES, ETC. WHEN WE DON'T USE CUBES FOR OTHER THINGS, THEY CAN BECOME GREAT STORAGE "CENTERS". THE ONES BELOW WERE BUILT BY KEN YOST FROM ½" PRESSBOARD.

WE'VE MENTIONED OUR FRIEND KEN YOST OFTEN IN THIS BOOK. THESE EXAMPLES SHOW HIS SUPERB FEELING FOR WOOD AS ONE OF THE MOST BENIGN MATERIALS TO LIVE WITH & WORK WITH. THE SIDEBOARD CONTAINS SIX AMPLE DRAWER UNITS FOR STORAGE. NOTE THE DROP-DOWN WORKING SURFACE. THE UNIT IS SCRIBED TO THE WALL & ELEVATING THE UNIT IN THIS MANNER TO WORKING HEIGHT HAS REDUCED OVERALL SIZE, MAKING IT EASIER TO DETACH & MOVE.

THE TABLE TO THE RIGHT IS REALLY A REJECT DOOR WITH AN ADDED FORMICA-COVERED BORDER AND LEGS.

IF YOU WANT CUSTOM-MADE & CUSTOM-DESIGNED NOMADIC FORMS & NOMADIC FURNITURE, CONTACT KEN:

＊ KEN YOST
24468 SHADELAND STREET
NEWHALL, CALIF. 91321, U.S.A.
(805) 255-0208

getting away from it all....

THE PRESSURES OF LIFE ARE INCREASING FOR US ALL. TO REMAIN STRONG, SENSITIVE, ABLE TO LOVE & CREATE, WE NEED A VITAL CENTER THAT REMAINS CALM. A PLACE AWAY FROM TELEPHONES, NEWSPAPERS, RADIOS & TELEVISION.

ANTOINE DE ST. EXUPÉRY FOUND IT AMONG NORTH AFRICAN DESERT SANDS & THE STARS [AS DID HIS "LITTLE PRINCE"]. THE JAPANESE BUILD A SPECIAL NICHE, _TOKONOMA_, TO HOLD ONE POEM ON A CALLIGRAPHIC SCROLL ["ONE MEETING, ONE CHANCE"] & A SPRAY OF PLUM BLOSSOMS. WE ALL SEEK A PRIVATE PLACE THAT MAKES CONTEMPLATION, MEDITATION & LOVE MORE POSSIBLE...

WHERE TO GO ALONE [OR WITH ONE OTHER] TO THINK, TO TALK, TO LISTEN TO VIVALDI'S _FOUR SEASONS_ OR TO HEAR CORNELIS VREESWIJK'S _SASKIA_ OR _LA FLÛTE DES ANDES_?

A PLACE FOR SEEING NATURE, BURNING JOSS & CANDLES, READING A POEM, PLAYING THE FLUTE...

IN OUR SOCIETIES PLACES LIKE THIS HAVE CEASED TO EXIST ➡ TO REMAIN SANE, WE MUST MAKE SOME!

AT THE TIME OF THIS WRITING [EARLY NOVEMBER 1973], THE SILLY SEASON HAS ERUPTED AGAIN: ACCORDING TO _TIME_ MAGAZINE, SOLITUDE IS FOR SALE IN TEXAS FOR

$80,000°° AND UP. THAT'S THE PRICE FOR A "CONTEMPLATIVE ENVIRONMENT" THAT CAN BE OUTFITTED WITH FILM SCREENS, A "STAND-UP BAR" [SIC], ISOMETRIC EXERCISE EQUIPMENT, ETC. & IS EQUIPPED WITH A SOFA THAT "GLIDES ON A TRACK AROUND THE PERIMETER, MOVING FROM THE AUDIO-VISUAL AREA, SAY, TO A WORK STATION." ARCHITECT WILLIAM PULGRAM, WHO PRESIDES OVER THE CONFECTING OF THESE TRIVIA, IS QUOTED:

"IT IS A RECOGNITION OF A NEED IN OUR SOCIETY, A SEARCH FOR 'THE REAL ME'." [TIME, Nov. 19, 1973, EUROPEAN EDITION].

➤ FORGET THE $80,000°° MINK-LINED WOMB! FIND WHAT YOUR OWN NEEDS REALLY ARE.

＊ YOU MAY BE LUCKY ENOUGH TO LOOK OUT OF YOUR WINDOW AT A BOTTLE-GREEN SKY MEETING THE SEA AND THE TUNDRA. SLED DOGS BARK & HOWL THROUGH YOUR VILLAGE, AND YOUR OWN HANDS ARE BUSY WITH THE MENDING OF FISHING SPEARS & NETS.

＊ OR YOU MAY LIE BACK AGAINST THE SUN-DRENCHED WALL OF YOUR PUEBLO. YOUR SON DRILLS THE CENTERS OF TURQUOISE & CHALCHIHUITL AND THE STEADY BEAT OF THE KACHINA DANCERS COMES FROM THE SQUARE.

＊ THE WIND RUSTLES THROUGH THE PINE TREES AS YOU LOOK AT THE MOON ABOVE

THE LAKE AT NIGHT. YOU SIT IN SAUNA, COMPLETELY AT PEACE, WITH THE SMELL OF BIRCH~WHISKS IN YOUR NOSE. SOON YOU'LL RACE STEAMING TO THE LAKE, TO BE EMBRACED BY THE ICY WATER.

＊SUNLIGHT BREAKS OVER THE DESERT. IT IS STILL COOL AS YOU HITCH UP YOUR ROBES FOR THE DAY'S JOURNEY. THE CAMELS SNORT AND THE AIR IS SO CLEAR THAT YOU CAN HEAR A VILLAGE DOG BARKING FROM MILES AWAY.

＊IT IS LATE AT NIGHT. THE LAST NOTES OF THE GAMELAN HAVE DIED AWAY. YOU DRINK A LAST GLASS OF *TUAK* AND RETURN TO THE VILLAGE. THERE YOU FIND THE LOVE OF THE PEOPLE YOU KNOW, AND THERE ARE NONE THAT YOU DO NOT KNOW. THERE IS ONLY A LONG "TODAY," A TIME-CONTINUUM OF BIRTHS AND DEATHS, MARRIAGES AND RITUALS, RAINS AND EARTHQUAKES.

➡ BUT MOST OF US WHO READ THIS BOOK HAVE NEVER LIVED THESE LIVES, OR ONLY FOR A FEW YEARS AT MOST. LACKING NATURE, LACKING CLOSE CONNECTION TO A LIFE-CYCLE, WE NEED A PLACE FOR BEING AT PEACE. BUT IN THIS AREA, NEEDS WILL BE RADICALLY DIFFERENT. YOU MUST INVENT FOR YOURSELF.

HENCE WE CANNOT GIVE YOU BUILDING PLANS FOR $80,000.00 PADS OR 80¢ CELLS. BUT HERE'S ONE ANYWAY:

A TREEHOUSE:
[SEEN FROM BELOW]

THESE DRAWINGS, ALL OF THE SAME TREEHOUSE, ARE JUST ONE POSSIBLE SUGGESTION:

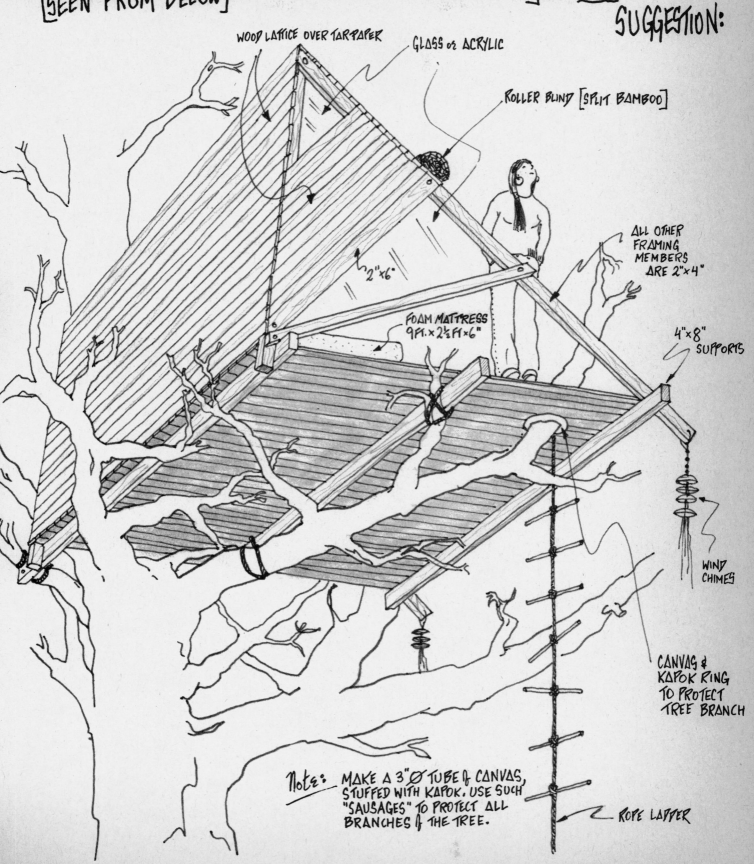

WOOD LATTICE OVER TARPAPER

GLASS OR ACRYLIC

ROLLER BLIND [SPLIT BAMBOO]

2"×6"

ALL OTHER FRAMING MEMBERS ARE 2"×4"

FOAM MATTRESS 9 FT. × 2⅓ FT × 6"

4"×8" SUPPORTS

WIND CHIMES

CANVAS & KAPOK RING TO PROTECT TREE BRANCH

Note: MAKE A 3"⌀ TUBE OF CANVAS, STUFFED WITH KAPOK. USE SUCH "SAUSAGES" TO PROTECT ALL BRANCHES OF THE TREE.

ROPE LADDER

LET YOUR TREE DICTATE THE SIZE & DESIGN of YOUR TREE-HOUSE.
THIS ONE WAS DESIGNED FOR METTE, WHO HAS A HANDSOME, OLD
& GNARLED TREE OVERLOOKING A SMALL LAKE NEAR ÅRHUS.
A 9FT × 9FT PLATFORM SITS IN THE MID-CROWN of THE TREE. IT
CONSISTS of FLOOR-BOARDS NAILED TO STURDY 4"×8"s THAT ARE
FIRMLY LASHED TO TREE-TRUNK & BRANCHES. THE UPPER
STRUCTURE IS MINIMAL: MOST of IT IS A DECK & ONE CAN
STAND UPRIGHT ONLY NEAR THE 6"-THICK FOAM PAD, WHICH IS
2½ FEET WIDE, RUNS THE ENTIRE WIDTH [9 FEET] & IS   CANVAS ~
COVERED.

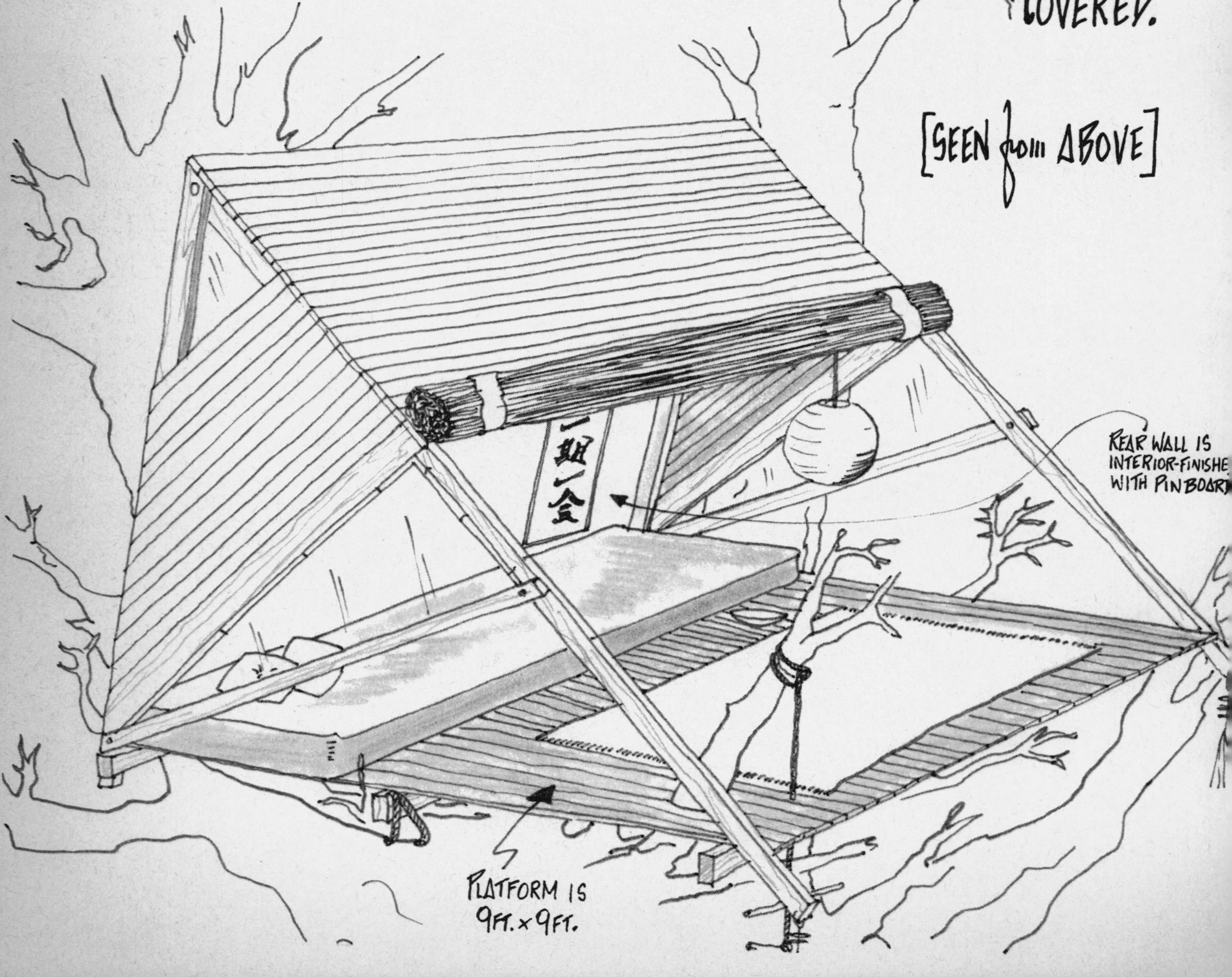

[SEEN from ABOVE]

一期一会

REAR WALL IS
INTERIOR-FINISHED
WITH PIN BOARD

PLATFORM IS
9 FT. × 9 FT.

THE CHINESE LANTERN IS <u>CANDLE-POWERED</u>. THERE IS
NO ELECTRICITY. IT IS A PLACE TO THINK, TO PLAN, TO WATCH THE
GOLDEN GRASSES AROUND THE POND WHIPPED BY OCTOBER WINDS AGAINST
THE LEADEN SKY. A PLACE TO MEDITATE, TO LOVE, TO WORK.

IF YOU LIVE IN THE CITY YOU CAN'T
HAVE A TREEHOUSE, BUT YOU STILL
<u>NEED</u> A REFUGE, AN OASIS.

YOU COULD BUILD
A CUBE [<u>NOMADIC</u>
<u>FURNITURE 1</u>, pp. 78-81] &
TURN IT INTO A
MEDITATION CUBE,
OR, OR, OR—<u>YOU</u>
<u>ARE THE DESIGNER</u>,
NOT WE!

DIAGRAMMATIC
SIDE VIEW of
TREEHOUSE

➡ BUT A PLACE TO
THINK & BE AT PEACE
IS A PRIME NEED. ⬅

"ALL MEN HAVE STARS, ... BUT THEY ARE NOT THE SAME THINGS FOR
DIFFERENT PEOPLE. FOR SOME, WHO ARE TRAVELLERS, THE STARS ARE
GUIDES. FOR OTHERS THEY ARE NO MORE THAN LIGHTS IN THE SKY...
BUT ALL THESE STARS ARE SILENT. YOU - YOU ALONE - WILL
HAVE THE STARS AS NO ONE ELSE HAS THEM...   "
"IT IS ONLY WITH THE HEART THAT ONE CAN SEE RIGHTLY; WHAT
IS ESSENTIAL IS INVISIBLE TO THE EYE."

[<u>THE LITTLE PRINCE</u>, ANTOINE DE SAINT-EXUPÉRY]

HINTS, INFO+MISC:

POSTAL LIMITS

IT MAKES LITTLE SENSE TO INCLUDE POSTAL RATES AS THESE CHANGE SO ABRUPTLY. HOWEVER, BOOKS AND OTHER ITEMS CAN BE SENT CHEAPLY BY SURFACE MAIL IF CERTAIN SIZE & WEIGHT LIMITS ARE MET. THESE LIMITS SEEM TO CHANGE ONLY RARELY, SO YOU MAY BE INTERESTED.

THE MAXIMUM PACKAGE [NON-BOOKS] IS 30 LBS. THESE BOXES HAVE TO BE NO BIGGER THAN: LENGTH + GIRTH (HEIGHT & WIDTH) → 82". SPECIAL RATES FOR A NUMBER OF BOXES GOING TO 1 ADDRESS. BOOKS: MAXIMUM 70 LBS, 100" LENGTH+GIRTH. THERE IS A 5LB OZ UNDER, 60"L+GIRTH RATE FOR SURFACE MAIL, AND A 5-30LB "PAL" SERVICE WILL GO AIRMAIL FOR $1.- EXTRA.

KEVI [44 RUGVÆNGET, DK-2630 TAASTRUP, DENMARK] PROBABLY MAKE THE BEST & HANDSOMEST ROLLER/CASTERS. THEY ARE SOLD IN SETS OF FOUR, COME IN MANY WEIGHT SUPPORTS & SIZES. THE COVERPLATES COME IN MATTE BLACK, WHITE, A ZIPPY RED, CHROME YELLOW.

BATHROOM SCALES ARE VERY VALUABLE PRODUCTS SINCE THEY CAN ALSO BE USED TO WEIGH BOXES & PACKAGES FOR SHIPPING OR MAILING, SUITCASES BEFORE FLYING, ETC. THIS PARTICULAR SCALE BY HANSON IS MADE OF UNUSUALLY TOUGH LEXAN, A FABULOUSLY "INDESTRUCTIBLE" PLASTIC.

Here is some information you might like to have about American and European voltages and what products might not work overseas.

1. Line voltage in the U.S. is 110 volts, alternating at 60 cycles (AC volts). Line voltage in Europe is 220 volts, alternating at 50 cycles (AC volts).

    FACT—It is clear from the above differences that U.S. electrical devices must use a converter of some type in order to operate in Europe and vice versa.

2. All producers of electricity in the U.S. alternate their voltage at the rate of 60 cycles per second, which the U.S. Bureau of Standards now enforces as a constant. The 60-cycle fluctuations can be used to control the speed of an electric motor and this principle is what keeps an electric clock running on time. This principle is also used to control the speed of record players, tape recorders and cassette players that run on AC voltage.

    FACT—Since 60 cycles is important in maintaining the speed of certain devices, these devices cannot be used in Europe where the rate is 50 cycles. (Electronic devices that can change the cycle rate exist but they are both complicated and expensive.)

3. There is an exception to the above fact. Devices that run on batteries often come with their own converters that allow the device to operate from a convenient wall outlet. These converters change the voltage from the wall to a safe, usable battery voltage and the converters are not affected by the difference in the cycle rate. This means you can use such devices in Europe by buying batteries for them, by buying a new converter for them, or by using your present U.S. converter and the one we show you how to build. You should *not* use these devices in Europe with the U.S. converter alone! You may burn out the device!

    FACT—There is an inexpensive converter you can make that will change the 220-volt European line voltage to the U.S. 110 volts. It produces a crude output and thus will only operate certain types of devices safely. If you shop around, you can make it yourself for under $5. Instructions are on the next page.

4. Below is a chart that, even though minimal, will answer 90% of the questions asked about what electrical products will work in Europe. The row on the left comprises those items that will work well with the circuit adaptor that we show you how to build. The second row lists all those products that you can use in Europe but that require a bulky, heavy TRANSFORMER in order to operate. A transformer (if you decide you can't live without one) should be purchased in Europe as they are too expensive to transport. Better yet, we suggest you give away or sell such items and buy their European counterparts. The last row of items in the chart cannot and will not work in Europe, so leave them home.

SIMPLE CONVERTER ITEMS (to make one, see next page)	TRANSFORMER ONLY	FORGET IT
any heating type device	anything with a motor	electric clocks
electric blankets	tube-type radios	clock radios
coffee percolators	tube-type hi-fi equip.	AC record
irons	mixers	players
toasters	can openers	AC recorders
frying pans and skillets	drills and other tools	AC cassettes
any battery-powered that	typewriters	timers (photo)
has its own converter	hair dryers	all TV sets

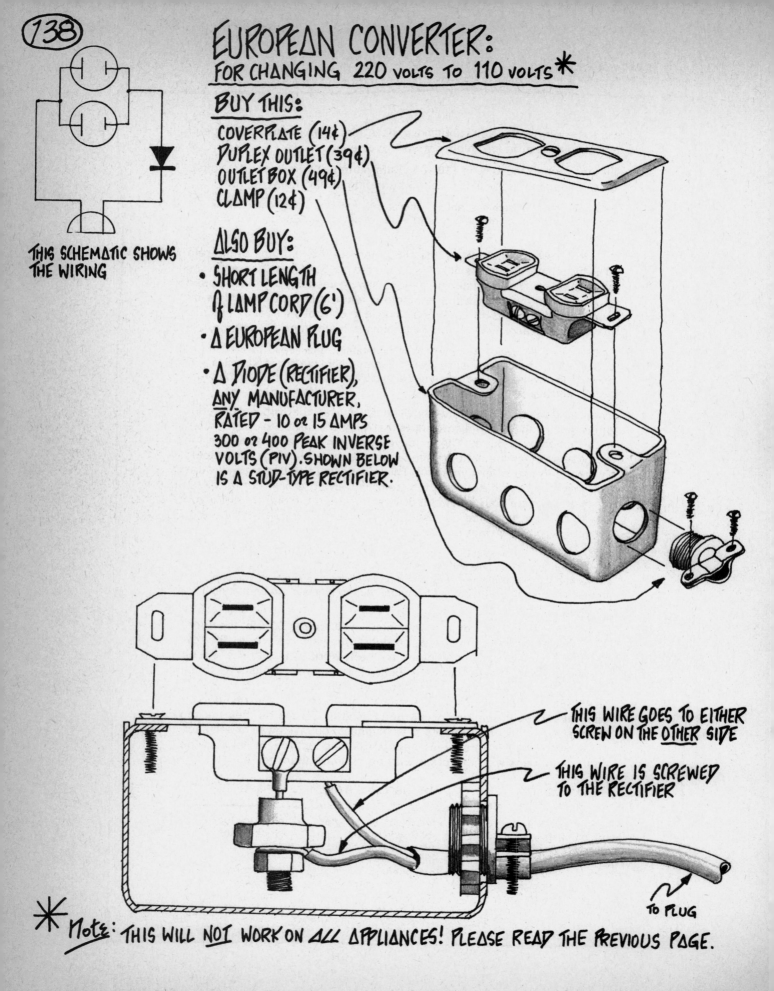

(138)

THIS SCHEMATIC SHOWS
THE WIRING

EUROPEAN CONVERTER:
FOR CHANGING 220 VOLTS TO 110 VOLTS *

BUY THIS:
COVERPLATE (14¢)
DUPLEX OUTLET (39¢)
OUTLET BOX (49¢)
CLAMP (12¢)

ALSO BUY:
• SHORT LENGTH OF LAMP CORD (6')
• A EUROPEAN PLUG
• A DIODE (RECTIFIER), ANY MANUFACTURER, RATED - 10 or 15 AMPS 300 or 400 PEAK INVERSE VOLTS (PIV). SHOWN BELOW IS A STUD-TYPE RECTIFIER.

THIS WIRE GOES TO EITHER SCREW ON THE OTHER SIDE

THIS WIRE IS SCREWED TO THE RECTIFIER

TO PLUG

* Note: THIS WILL NOT WORK ON ALL APPLIANCES! PLEASE READ THE PREVIOUS PAGE.

"THINNEST" ELECTRONIC CALCULATOR:

Actual size

Sinclair Executive

WHEN THE "SINCLAIR EXECUTIVE" [SHOWN TO THE RIGHT IN ACTUAL SIZE] FIRST MADE ITS APPEARANCE, THE BRITISH MAGAZINE <u>DESIGN</u> PANNED IT AS A "RICH MAN'S PLAYTHING". THE MANUFACTURERS, HELPED BY DEMAND FOR THEIR UNIT, MANAGED TO LOWER THE PRICE BY MORE THAN 50%. THE UNIT IS ULTRA~SLIM [THE INSTRUCTION BOOKLET THAT COMES WITH IT IS THICKER!], LIGHTWEIGHT & EASILY SLIPS INTO A POCKET. IT IS POWERED BY TINY HEARING-AID BATTERIES AND FEATURES FLOATING DECIMAL, "CONSTANT," AND WILL EASILY ADD, SUBTRACT, MULTIPLY, DIVIDE, DO CURRENCY CONVERSIONS, COMPOUND INTEREST,ETC., ETC.

IT HAS [IN BRITAIN] RECEIVED THE 1973 DESIGN COUNCIL AWARD.

AN UNUSUALLY NOMADIC PIECE. VIC FINDS IT INVALUABLE [& LIGHTER THAN A WALLET] WHEN FLYING ➤ IT WILL DO SIMPLE NAVIGATIONAL COMPUTATIONS.

➤ SINCLAIR RADIONICS, LTD.
LONDON ROAD, ST. IVES, HUNTINGDONSHIRE,
PE 17 4HJ ENGLAND

HEATHKIT:

THE HEATHKIT PEOPLE OF BENTON HARBOR, MICHIGAN [U.S.A], MAKE THE BEST ELECTRONIC KITS ON THE GLOBE. WE SHOW YOU TWO OF THEIR CALCULATORS [KITS] BECAUSE OF THEIR IMMEDIATE USEFULNESS TO NOMADICS. [YOU'VE GOT TO KEEP TABS ON HOW MUCH MONEY YOU'RE SAVING, RIGHT?] ACTUALLY, THE DESK MODEL IS PERFECT FOR BILLS AND CHECKBOOK UPKEEP, FIGURING MATERIAL NEEDED FOR A <u>NOMADIC FURNITURE</u> PROJECT, ETC.

    THIS MODEL HAS A FULL 8-DIGIT READOUT, WITH FLOATING OR FIXED DECIMAL POINT. IT WILL READ IN A CONSTANT NUMBER [MATHS: $\pi = 3.1416$ OR MONEY CONVERSION: (U.S.) \$1^{00} = DM 2^{41}, ETC.] & THE CONSTANT WILL STAY IN ITS "MEMORY" WHILE YOU USE IT TO MULTIPLY OR DIVIDE WITH A STRING OF NUMBERS.

    THE ELECTRONICS GO TOGETHER WITH NO DIFFICULTY & THE INSTRUCTION MANUAL EVEN INCLUDES TROUBLE-SHOOTING CHARTS [IN CASE SOMETHING GOES ASTRAY]. THE ONLY SKILL NEEDED IS SOLDERING, WHICH IS REALLY EASY. A PRINTED CIRCUIT BOARD SPEEDS ASSEMBLY.

THE HEATHKIT POCKET PORTABLE HAS ALL THE FEATURES OF THE DESK UNIT,
EXCEPT THAT IT OPERATES ON
RECHARGEABLE BATTERIES.
SARA TAKES IT TO THE SHOPS
& TALLIES NOT ONLY THE BILL
BUT ALSO "COST-PER-UNIT"
SAVINGS OF ONE PRODUCT
COMPARED WITH ANOTHER.
THE HENNESSEYS FEEL THEY
HAVE PAID FOR THE CALCULATOR
IN FOOD SAVINGS ALONE IN
JUST A FEW MONTHS.

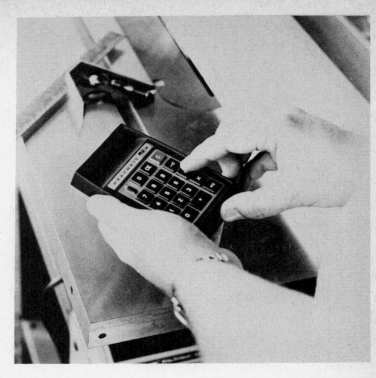

Consumer's Note

NOMADIC NOTE: IN ADDITION TO QUALITY, ONE REASON WE ARE SOLD
ON HEATHKIT EQUIPMENT IS THAT 90% OF IT CAN BE WIRED EITHER FOR
AMERICAN or EUROPEAN VOLTAGES. THAT MEANS THE STUFF DOESN'T
BECOME USELESS WHEN MOVING. BOTH CALCULATORS CAN BE WIRED &
REWIRED THIS WAY. Heath also make a large amount of other electronic
items too vast to   write for a catalog!
detail here.

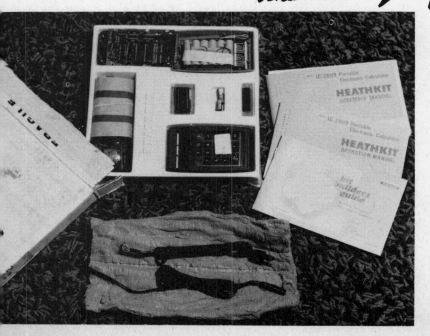

THIS IS THE WAY THE POCKET
CALCULATOR IS PACKAGED
IN KIT FORM. THE LARGE
VACUUM-FORMED CONTAINER
SERVES AS A CONVENIENT
PARTS TRAY WHILE BUILDING.
HEATHKIT IS NOT CHEAP.
THEY SELL TOP-OF-THE-LINE
ELECTRONICS AT KIT PRICES
—BUT WORTH EVERY PENNY.

SNAP-TOGETHER TOTE TRAY:

THIS SIMPLE, ONE-EVENING PROJECT CAN BE DONE EASILY W/A SABRE SAW, HAND SAW OR ROUTER. ORIGINALLY JIM DESIGNED IT FOR TOOLS & MADE IT OF ⅜" PLYWOOD. BUT YOU CAN EASILY ADAPT THE PLANS TO FOAMCORE OR HEAVY CARDBOARD FOR LIGHTER THINGS, SEWING STORAGE, ETC. BUT REMEMBER THAT THE SLOTS WILL BECOME SMALLER AS THE MATERIAL BECOMES THINNER. ➡ LOOK AT THE PHOTOS: ASSEMBLY STARTS WITH THE HANDLE AND BOTTOM. AFTER INSERTING AND TWISTING THEM 90°, THEY BECOME LOCKED WITH THE 2 END PIECES. THESE SHOULD BE BENT CAREFULLY OUTWARD TO CLEAR THE TAB ON THE BOTTOM UNTIL THE TAB FITS INTO THE MATCHING SLOT ON THE END PIECE. THE SIDES ARE MOUNTED THE SAME WAY. BESIDES USING NO GLUE OR FASTENERS, THESE TOTE TRAYS ARE MUCH CHEAPER THAN THEIR MANUFACTURED [NON-NOMADIC] COUNTERPARTS.
THE WOOD [EVEN IN OCTOBER 1973] COST LESS THAN 50¢.

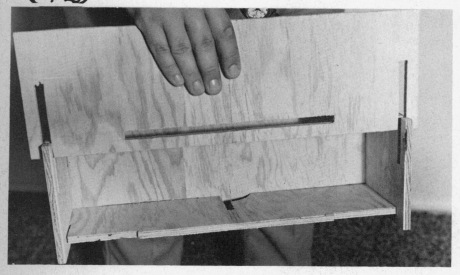

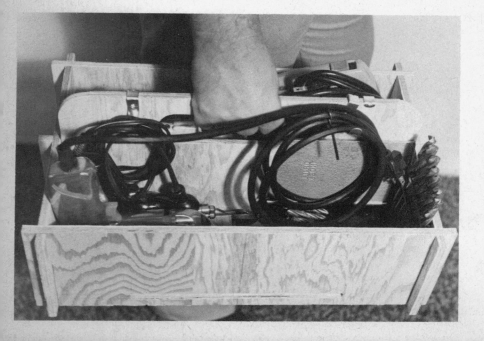

(142)

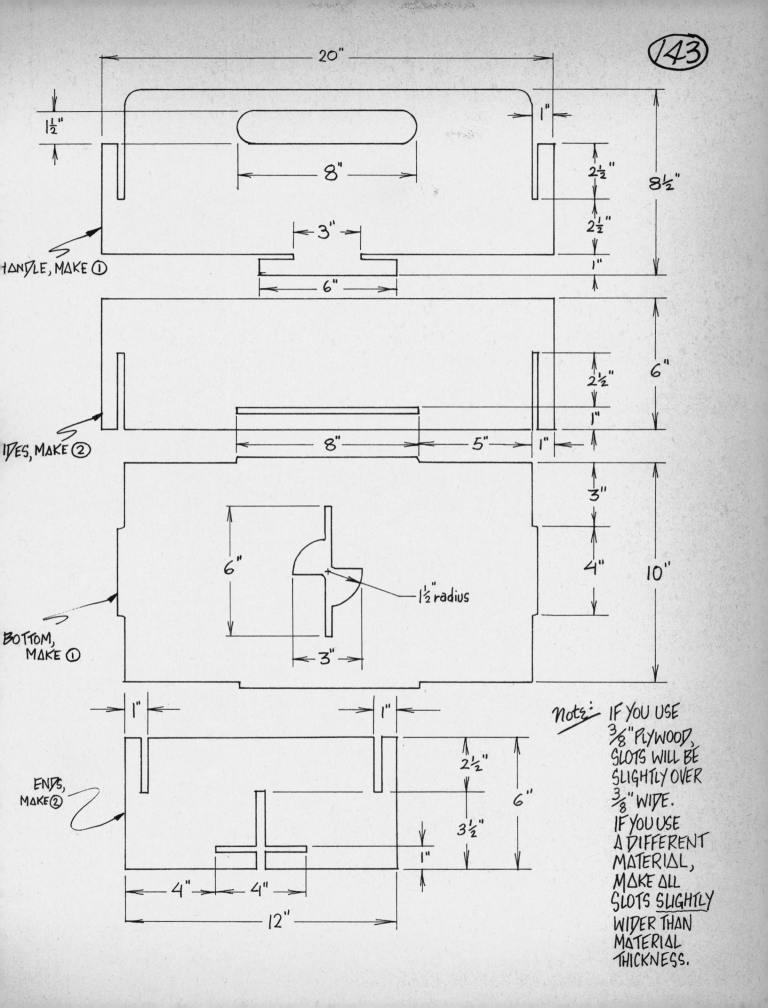

20"

1½"

1"

8"

2½"

2½"

8½"

3"

1"

6"

HANDLE, MAKE ①

6"

2½"

1"

8"

5"

1"

SIDES, MAKE ②

3"

6"

4"

10"

6"

1½" radius

3"

BOTTOM,
MAKE ①

1"

1"

2½"

6"

3½"

1"

ENDS,
MAKE ②

4"

4"

12"

Note: IF YOU USE
⅜" PLYWOOD,
SLOTS WILL BE
SLIGHTLY OVER
⅜" WIDE.
IF YOU USE
A DIFFERENT
MATERIAL,
MAKE ALL
SLOTS SLIGHTLY
WIDER THAN
MATERIAL
THICKNESS.

TOOLS + MATERIALS:

<u>Note</u>: There is an energy & materials crisis: <u>rent or borrow</u> power tools: buy only if you really must! Hand tools are listed in our earlier book.

SABRE SAW
BEST ALL-AROUND TOOL. NOT TOO ACCURATE ON STRAIGHT LINES. MAKES ROUGH BUT INTRICATE CUTS. *LOOK FOR THE LEAST SHAFT-WOBBLE IF YOU BUY ONE.*

CIRCULAR SAW
PERFECT FOR TEARING INTO LARGE PLYWOOD PANELS. STRAIGHT-CUTTING ONLY!

HAND DRILL
INDISPENSABLE! GET A <u>VARIABLE SPEED</u>/ REVERSIBLE – COSTS MORE, BUT WORTH IT.

ROUTER
WILL DO ALMOST <u>ANYTHING</u> WITH PRECISION & GREAT ACCURACY. GET ¾ HP or BIGGER. *FIRST GET A BOOK ON ROUTERS AND SEE ALL IT CAN DO!*

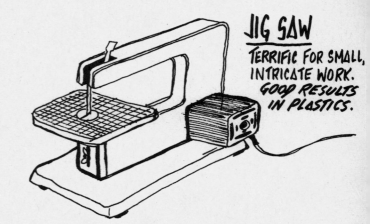

JIG SAW
TERRIFIC FOR SMALL, INTRICATE WORK. *GOOD RESULTS IN PLASTICS.*

ORBITAL/STRAIGHT SANDER
GENERAL USE. *BUY MEDIUM-PRICED UNIT!* LOW-COST ONES WEAR OUT QUICKLY.

FINISHING SANDER
ORBITAL ACTION ONLY. FOR SMOOTH FINISHING OF VENEERS, ETC.

BELT SANDER
DESIGNED FOR *FAST* CUTTING OF ALL MATERIALS, INCLUDING SOFT METALS. USUALLY POWERFUL & HEAVY.

RADIAL-ARM SAW

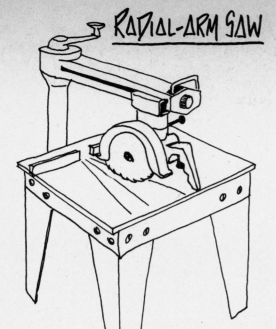

TABLE SAW

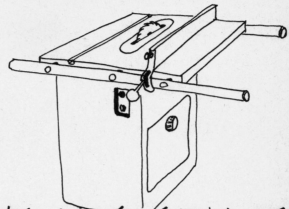

IN CHOOSING BETWEEN THESE TWO, FOLLOW YOUR PREFERENCE. MOST PROFESSIONALS PREFER A GOOD TABLE SAW. ADMITTEDLY THE RADIAL-ARM SAW CAN DO MORE "TRICKS" & IS SOMEWHAT LESS EXPENSIVE. HOWEVER, THE TABLE SAW IS MORE ACCURATE [ESPECIALLY FOR TRUE MITRES] & IS SOMEWHAT SAFER TOO.

LINEAR LUMBER

ASK FOR:	TRUE SIZE:
1×2	3/4" × 1 1/2"
1×3	3/4" × 2 1/2"
1×4	3/4" × 3 1/2"
1×6	3/4" × 5 1/2"
1×8	3/4" × 7 1/4"
1×10	3/4" × 9 1/4"
1×12	3/4" × 11 1/4"
2×2	1 1/2" × 1 1/2"
2×4	1 1/2" × 3 1/2"
2×6	1 1/2" × 5 1/2"
4×4	3 1/2" × 3 1/2"

SHEET LUMBER

THICKNESSES

1/4" PLY, FINNPLY, CHIPBD., MASONITE

1/2" PLY, FINNPLY, CHIPBD., MASONITE

3/4" PLY, FINNPLY, CHIPBD.

SIZES

4×4 ft. or 48"×48"

4×8 ft. or 48"×96"

5 ft×5 ft FINNPLY ONLY

MISC. SCRAP SIZES

36" DOWEL RODS

1/8"	DIAMETER
1/4"	"
3/8"	"
1/2"	"
5/8"	"
*3/4"	"
7/8"	"
1 1/4"	"

*1", 1 1/2" & 2" DIAMETER
*ALSO IN 8, 10 & 12 FOOT LENGTHS

These charts are a necessary repeat from NOMADIC FURNITURE 1

NOTES & CALCULATIONS:

148 NOTES & CALCULATIONS:

NOTES & CALCULATIONS:

＊

Note: HOW TO ORDER FROM OUTSIDE THE U.S.A.: All OF THE MANUFACTURERS & SHOPS LISTED IN THIS BOOK WILL BE PLEASED TO SHIP TO YOU. YOU CAN PAY VIA INTERNATIONAL MONEY ORDER [BUY THIS AT YOUR BANK]. REMEMBER THAT WITH THE CURRENT CURRENCY FLUCTUATION, INTERNATIONAL INFLATION & THE ENERGY CRISIS → PRICES WILL CHANGE CONTINUALLY! SHIPPING TO NEW YORK FROM, SAY, COPENHAGEN, CAN TAKE 4-6 WEEKS BY SURFACE MAIL, 3 DAYS VIA AIR-FREIGHT, WHICH COSTS MUCH MORE, OF COURSE. SEE ALSO PAGES 8, 9 & 184 IN THE CATALOGUE OF CATALOGUES BY MARIA ELENA DE LA IGLESIA (RANDOM HOUSE, 1972) FOR MORE SHIPPING & SHOPPING INFO.

Photographic Credits:

WE WISH TO THANK THE MANUFACTURERS, PERIODICAL PUBLISHERS & PHOTOGRAPHERS WHOSE MATERIAL APPEARS IN THIS BOOK. HERE ARE OUR SOURCES:

P. 56, 57: DANILO ALEGRI, COURTESY: ABITARE MAGAZINE, ITALY
P. 74-76: YALE GREENFIELD
P. 72: ANA PULLINEN, COURTESY: TRESTON OY, FINLAND
P. 90-91: AASE RAAGAARD
P. 122, 123: "ROBOTS S.A.S." COURTESY: ABITARE
P. 110, 111: CARREBYE FOTOGRAFI A.S., COURTESY: CADO, DENMARK
P. 12*, 14, 16, 73, 74, 79, 82, 84, 102: VICTOR PAPANEK
            * WITH HELP FROM WINKLER FOTOGRAFI
P. 24, 49, 60-65, 68, 85, 88, 89, 96, 97, 99, 112, 117, 121, 126-129, 140-142: SARA J. HENNESSEY

ALL OTHER PHOTOS ARE FROM MANUFACTURERS' CATALOGS & ADVERTISEMENTS IN DENMARK, ITALY, SWEDEN, THE U.S. & THE U.K.

SPECIAL THANKS TO HENRIK MIKKELSEN OF KØBENHAVN WHO HELPED WITH IDEAS AND IN BUILDING EXPERIMENTAL PROTOTYPES.

ABOUT THE AUTHORS

Victor Papanek is a UNESCO International Design Expert. He studied at Cooper Union, at M.I.T., and with Frank Lloyd Wright. He is the author of numerous articles and of *Design for the Real World: Human Ecology and Social Change,* and is now teaching design in London.

James Hennessey is Assistant Dean at the School of Design at the California Institute of the Arts at Valencia.